THE DECADES OF TWENTIETH-CENTURY AMERICA

AMERICA IN THE 1940s

EDMUND LINDOP

with MARGARET J. GOLDSTEIN

Twenty-First Century Books · Minneapolis

Twenty-First Century Books
A division of Lerner Publishing Group, Inc.
241 First Avenue North
Minneapolis, MN 55401 U.S.A.

Website address: www.lernerbooks.com

Library of Congress Cataloging-in-Publication Data

Lindop, Edmund.
    America in the 1940s / by Edmund Lindop with Margaret J. Goldstein.
        p.   cm. — (The decades of twentieth-century America)
    Includes bibliographical references and index.
    ISBN 978–0–7613–2945–9 (lib. bdg. : alk. paper)
    1. United States—History—1933–1945—Juvenile literature. 2. United States—History—1945–1953—Juvenile literature. 3. Nineteen forties—Juvenile literature. I. Title.
    E806.L5655 2010
    973.917—dc22   2007042904

Manufactured in the United States of America
1 2 3 4 5 6 – PA – 15 14 13 12 11 10

CONTENTS

★★★★★★★★★★★★★★★★★

Unemployed men wait in line for food in New York City in 1932.
THE GREAT DEPRESSION (1929–1942) was marked by widespread unemployment.

HARD TIMES

Franklin D. Roosevelt had a tough job on his hands. In 1932 he won the U.S. presidential election. His campaign song was "Happy Days Are Here Again." But singing about happy days didn't make it so. When Roosevelt took office, the United States was in the grip of the Great Depression. Millions of Americans—almost 25 percent of the workforce—were unemployed. Banks and other businesses had shut down. Farmers had gone broke. Thousands of farm families took to the road, looking for work. In cities some people lived in makeshift shacks. In rural areas, they lived in tent camps. Many people went hungry. It was a bleak, desperate time.

On the campaign trail, Roosevelt had promised to end the Depression and to bring the nation out of poverty. Once in office, he created a massive government program called the New Deal. Under the New Deal, the federal government attacked poverty on many fronts. The government passed laws that helped stabilize banking, farming, business, and the economy. New Deal agencies hired thousands of workers to build highways, bridges, parks, dams, courthouses, and schools. They hired artists, photographers, and writers to document life in the United States. The government passed the Social Security Act, which guaranteed an income for the elderly, the disabled, and other needy Americans.

The New Deal relieved the suffering of many poor and hungry Americans. But it did not end the Great Depression. Throughout the 1930s, the U.S. economy remained in a slump. By the end of the decade, unemployment had decreased to 15 percent—but that was still too high. "There were no jobs of any kind to be had," remembered Marjorie Cartwright. "I lived in Clarksburg, West Virginia, a small town—around forty thousand people. The factories were working with skeleton crews, and no one was hiring." Americans feared that the Depression would never end.

■ STORM IN EUROPE

Although Roosevelt hadn't solved their money problems, Americans loved him. They overwhelmingly elected him to a second term in 1936. Roosevelt continued working to improve the nation's economy. He also turned his attention overseas.

In Germany Adolf Hitler and his Nazi Party had come to power in the 1930s. Hitler was a vicious and fanatical dictator. He wanted to rid Germany of Jews and other "undesirables," including Gypsies, homosexuals, and disabled people. He also wanted to conquer Europe. In Italy another dictator, Benito Mussolini, had risen to power. Both Hitler and Mussolini created Fascist governments. In a Fascist system, the government has complete control over politics, culture, society, and the economy.

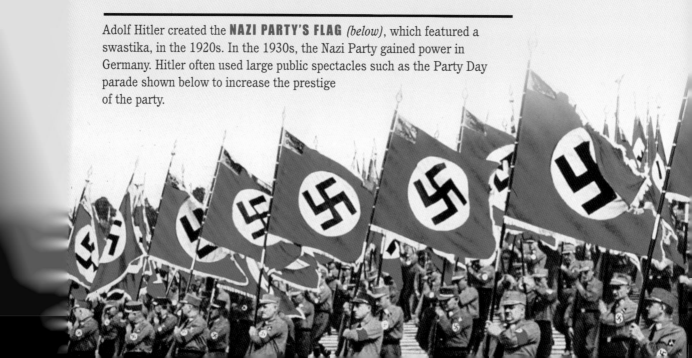

Adolf Hitler created the **NAZI PARTY'S FLAG** *(below)*, which featured a swastika, in the 1920s. In the 1930s, the Nazi Party gained power in Germany. Hitler often used large public spectacles such as the Party Day parade shown below to increase the prestige of the party.

PRESIDENT FRANKLIN ROOSEVELT in 1937

In Japan, military leaders controlled the government. They wanted to take over Asia and the islands of the Pacific Ocean. In 1936 Germany and Italy made a military alliance. Japan signed treaties with these two European nations. The world watched warily.

On September 1, 1939, Hitler invaded and quickly overpowered Poland. Two days later, Britain and France, two of the most powerful nations in Europe, declared war on Germany. World War II (1939–1945) had begun.

■ ISOLATION OR INTERVENTION?

What would the United States do? At first most Americans were opposed to entering the war in Europe. The United States had fought side by side with the British and the French in World War I (1914–1918) and had sustained heavy casualties. Most Americans wanted no part in another bloodbath in Europe.

In the late 1930s, Congress passed a series of neutrality acts. These laws were designed to keep the United States out of another war. The laws banned the U.S. sale and transportation of military equipment and forbade the United States to make loans to warring nations. Politicians and many others argued that the United States should mind its own business and leave the Europeans to fight their own war.

President Roosevelt, on the other hand, believed that the United States should fight the Germans. He argued that dictators such as Hitler and Mussolini were a threat to democratic societies everywhere on Earth. Although many disagreed with Roosevelt, Americans still trusted and supported him.

President Roosevelt had guided the nation through the grim years of the Great Depression—a time of sacrifice and fear. If the United States were to enter the war in Europe, Americans would have to sacrifice again. That was the prospect facing the nation as the calendar turned and December 31, 1939, became January 1, 1940.

7

Explosions wrack Hickam Field during the Japanese attack on
PEARL HARBOR, HAWAII, on December 7, 1941.

CHAPTER ONE

"REMEMBER PEARL HARBOR":

WORLD WAR II

A s 1940 began, World War II raged in Europe. In the spring of that year, Germany marched into Norway, Denmark, Belgium, the Netherlands (Holland), and France. On its own, Great Britain tried to survive against a German bombing onslaught. Meanwhile, Japan joined the German–Italian military alliance. The three nations, called the Axis powers, pledged to support one another's military campaigns.

Officially, the United States still remained neutral. But it did take steps to prepare for war. The federal government began to buy planes, ships, and tanks. Altering earlier neutrality acts, it sent weapons and equipment to help the British. The U.S. government also created the Selective Service System to draft men into military service.

Japan, meanwhile, had been conquering its neighbors, including large portions of China and Southeast Asia. As Japanese forces threatened the Pacific, the United States grew more and more alarmed. Relations between Japan and the United States went from bad to worse.

■ SNEAK ATTACK

On December 7, 1941, the Japanese made a surprise attack. With ships, airplanes, and more than fifteen thousand men, the Japanese struck the U.S. naval base at Pearl Harbor, Hawaii. U.S. losses were staggering. Of the eight U.S.

9

battleships in the harbor that day, four capsized or sank. The remaining four ships suffered heavy damage. The attack also destroyed 108 U.S. airplanes on the ground. Worse yet, about twenty-four hundred Americans were killed. About two thousand were wounded.

The next day, President Roosevelt, who had been elected to an unprecedented third term the year before, addressed Congress: "Yesterday, December 7, 1941—a date which will live in infamy—the United States of America was suddenly and deliberately attacked by naval and air forces of Japan." The president asked Congress for an official declaration of war against Japan. He promised, "No matter how long it may take us to overcome this premeditated invasion, the American people in their righteous might, will win through to absolute victory."

The U.S. Senate voted unanimously for war. In the House of Representatives, the vote was 388 to 1 (with only Jeannette Rankin of Montana, the first woman elected to Congress, casting a no vote). Immediately, Great Britain, Canada, and China (allies of the United States) also declared war on Japan.

On December 11, Japan's allies, Germany and Italy, declared war on the United States. The conflict had become global.

Americans were immediately united in their desire to defeat the Axis. The United States put its war machine into high gear. Men joined the military by the tens of thousands. U.S. factories began churning out guns and ammunition. The United States had to fight on two fronts—Europe and the Pacific. The entire nation readied itself for a long, hard fight.

President Franklin D. Roosevelt signs the **DECLARATION OF WAR AGAINST JAPAN** on December 8, 1941.

> **❝ Yesterday, December 7, 1941—a date which will live in infamy—the United States of America was suddenly and deliberately attacked by naval and air forces of Japan. ❞**

—*President Franklin D. Roosevelt, December 8, 1941*

■ BAD NEWS IN THE PACIFIC

The Japanese had a daring war plan: First, cripple the U.S. Pacific Fleet at Pearl Harbor. Then, before the United States was able to strike back, move rapidly to seize territory in Southeast Asia.

The plan worked perfectly. After knocking out half the U.S. fleet at Pearl Harbor, the Japanese captured Malaya (modern-day Malaysia). They drove the British out of Singapore and Hong Kong and took over Java and Sumatra in the Dutch East Indies (modern-day Indonesia). Then the entire continent of Australia was exposed to Japanese invasion.

Australia looked to its ally the United States for help. But these first months of the war were a dark time for Americans. The Japanese advance seemed unstoppable. U.S. forces lost battle after battle. Seven hundred U.S. Marines defended the island of Guam, a U.S. outpost in the Pacific. A six-thousand-man Japanese force landed on the island on December 10, 1941, and captured it two days later. On tiny Wake Island, four hundred U.S. Marines fought heroically for fifteen days before being overwhelmed.

In the Philippines, Japanese forces bottled up General Douglas MacArthur's U.S. forces on the peninsula of Bataan. President Roosevelt ordered MacArthur to abandon his forces and go to Australia. Promising "I shall return," MacArthur left behind thousands of U.S. and Filipino troops. Under MacArthur's successor, General Jonathan Wainwright, the defenders fought on with great courage. But isolated, starving, and ravaged by tropical diseases, they finally surrendered to the Japanese.

Surrender brought no relief to the sick and starving men. The Japanese started them on a nightmare trip that became known as the Bataan Death March. Already dazed and weak from thirst and starvation, the prisoners were driven relentlessly forward under a blistering sun. The march became a horror of blazing heat, thirst, hunger, and cruel treatment by the enemy guards. Thousands died from

U.S. prisoners of war carry fellow soldiers who have fallen during the **BATAAN DEATH MARCH** in 1942.

disease or exhaustion. Many were shot by the guards when they fell by the way. About seventy-five thousand men began the 65-mile (104-kilometer) march. Only fifty-four thousand were alive when it ended at a prisoner of war camp. The story of the brutal Bataan Death March shocked and angered the United States and hardened its resolve to defeat Japan.

■ BACK ON TOP

General MacArthur, with orders to protect Australia, based his defense at the little town of Port Moresby, Papua New Guinea, off the northeastern coast of Australia. In May 1942, Japanese warships sailed toward this U.S. base. U.S. naval intelligence had broken the secret Japanese codes and knew of the coming invasion. Admiral Chester W. Nimitz ordered U.S. naval forces to intercept the Japanese fleet in the Coral Sea. The U.S. fleet included two big aircraft carriers, *Yorktown* and *Lexington*.

For two days, the two sides fought a unique battle in which the ships never came close enough to exchange fire. The battle was fought entirely by planes launched from the aircraft carriers. U.S. planes sank the great Japanese carrier *Soho* and damaged two others. They also sank a Japanese destroyer. For the first time, the Japanese offensive in the Pacific was stopped.

The Japanese decided to make a dramatic move by launching a single, decisive attack. As a target, they selected the little-known island of Midway, about 1,000 miles (1,609 km) northwest of Hawaii. More than one hundred Japanese warships steamed eastward from Japan, across 2,000 miles (3,218 km) of ocean.

The plan depended on surprise. But again, U.S. naval intelligence had decoded Japan's secret messages. U.S. cruisers and destroyers, as well as three big aircraft carriers, lay in wait. When the Japanese arrived on June 4, 1942, U.S. forces took them by complete surprise.

As at the Coral Sea, planes did all the fighting. The battle raged for four days. In the end, U.S. forces were victorious. They sank four Japanese aircraft carriers and crippled three Japanese battleships.

The U.S. victory at Midway marked a turning point in the Pacific. Japan suddenly found itself on the defensive for the first time in the war. From that moment, U.S. forces were on the attack, moving relentlessly toward Japan.

The push began on August 7, 1942, when U.S. Marines landed on Guadalcanal in the Solomon Islands. Island fighting posed many hazards: steamy heat, drenching rains, rats, and bugs. Some marines contracted malaria or dysentery. Their feet were constantly wet and sometimes broke out in "jungle rot." One GI (soldier) remembered the landscape on Guadalcanal:

> Jungle was really rough. We were hit by heat, mosquitoes, leeches, and a little bit of everything else. . . . Some vines grew as wide as your leg. We called them "Wait-a-Minute Vines." They had big hooks on them like a rooster spur . . . like a razor. I still have scars from them. . . . Mosquitoes were so thick you could wipe them off your arms in handfuls. You wade through the rivers and you'd come out with leeches. . . . You'd look down and there was this creature on your leg full of blood.

Worst of all were enemy soldiers, who came charging out of the jungle at night in wild suicide raids. In February 1943, after six months of bloody fighting, Americans finally won control of Guadalcanal.

> **" Jungle was really rough. We were hit by heat, mosquitoes, leeches, and a little bit of everything else."**

—U.S. Marine on Guadalcanal, August 1942

■ ISLAND HOPPING

After Guadalcanal, the Allies (the nations fighting the Axis) continued to steadily win back the Pacific. In a strategy of "island hopping," they took one island after another, moving westward toward Japan. In fierce fighting, U.S. forces captured the Marianas Islands, including the island of Guam.

In late 1944, General MacArthur returned to the Philippines. There, in the Battle of Leyte Gulf, the Japanese unleashed a deadly new weapon: kamikaze (suicide) planes. Each plane carried a 550-pound (249-kilogram) bomb. The pilot's mission was to crash-land his plane on a U.S. aircraft carrier, blowing himself up and also sinking the ship. The kamikaze fighters inflicted great damage, but the Allies won a major victory at Leyte Gulf.

In February 1945, U.S. troops reached Manila, the Philippine capital, and freed five thousand Allied prisoners there. It took another month to liberate Manila. Fighting became a house-to-house struggle, as twenty thousand Japanese fought almost to the last man.

U.S. forces then turned north to the islands of Iwo Jima and Okinawa. Iwo Jima is a small and barren volcanic island, 775 miles (1,246 km) from Honshu, the main island of Japan. More than twenty thousand Japanese troops defended the island. The U.S. Marines took it inch by inch, in some of the fiercest fighting of the war. Only 350 miles (563 km) from mainland Japan, Okinawa was of great strategic importance. The Allies wanted it as a jumping-off point from which to invade Japan. After weeks of bloody battles, Okinawa fell to U.S. forces.

At the same time, U.S. fighter pilots raided Japanese cities. Their planes carried firebombs, which burned factories, docks, and other structures when they hit. One by one, Japan's big cities—Tokyo (the capital), Nagoya, Kobe, and Osaka—were devastated.

During the early years of World War II, Allied intelligence broke secret German and Japanese codes. The Japanese, in turn, broke every code the Americans devised. The U.S. military desperately needed a code that could not be broken.

Military veteran Philip Johnston remembered that U.S. forces had used a Native American language—Choctaw—to send secret messages across German lines during World War I. The Germans had intercepted the messages but could not understand a single word. The child of missionaries (religious workers), Johnston had grown up on the Navajo Reservation in Arizona. He spoke the Navajo language fluently. Because Navajo is a complex, unwritten language, Johnston believed it could be the undecipherable code the U.S. military needed in World War II.

Early in 1942, Johnston demonstrated his idea to U.S. Marine officers. Navajo volunteers translated a military message from English into Navajo. In another room, other Navajos translated the same message back into English. The whole process took twenty seconds. To encode, transmit, and decode the same message by machine would have taken thirty minutes.

Convinced, the marines immediately enlisted twenty-nine Navajo recruits. In May 1942, they created the Navajo code. They developed a dictionary and assigned Navajo words to represent more than four hundred frequently used military terms. For example, the Navajo term *besh-lo* (which means "iron fish") was the code word for "submarine." *Dah-he-tih-hi* (hummingbird) was code for "fighter plane." *Jay-sho* (buzzard) meant "bomber."

The code talkers, as the Navajo speakers were called, memorized all the code words and then shipped out for the Pacific. In all, about 420 Navajos served as marine code talkers. They transmitted vital messages by telephone and radio. The code talkers took part in every major battle in the Pacific. At Iwo Jima, six code talkers worked around the clock during the first two days of the battle. They sent and received more than eight hundred messages, all without error. The Japanese never broke the Navajo code.

15

CORPORAL HENRY BAHE JR. *(LEFT)* **AND PRIVATE FIRST CLASS GEORGE H. KIRK** send a message in Navajo code from close to the front lines in the Pacific.

■ ACROSS THE ATLANTIC

As U.S. troops battled in the Pacific, others crossed the Atlantic Ocean to help the Allies in Europe. From air bases in Great Britain, U.S. pilots pounded targets in Germany. U.S. naval forces battled with German U-boats (submarines) in the Atlantic.

In November 1942, U.S. troops under General Dwight D. Eisenhower invaded North Africa to fight German and Italian forces there. Battles raged throughout the winter of 1943. The Allies finally prevailed in May.

Using North Africa as a base, in July 1943, Allied troops struck at the island of Sicily, off the southern tip of Italy. On September 9, they invaded the Italian mainland against stiff resistance. After heavy fighting, the Allies finally captured Rome, the Italian capital, on June 4, 1944.

For the Allies, the most important target was Germany—the seat of Nazi power. Striking at Germany would require a massive invasion of Europe. The Allies planned to make the assault in Normandy, a region of northwestern France.

Allied leaders chose General Eisenhower to oversee the invasion, nicknamed Operation Overlord. His orders were as follows: "You will enter the continent of Europe and, in conjunction with the other United Nations, undertake operations aimed at the heart of Germany and the destruction of her armed forces."

As a base for Eisenhower's forces, much of southern England was transformed into a giant training camp. Roads thronged with marching men. The air cracked with the sounds of soldiers testing their weapons. The encampment included bulldozers, power plants, radio stations, medical units, kitchens, bakeries, and laundries to support the invasion force.

> **❝ You will enter the continent of Europe and, in conjunction with the other United Nations, undertake operations aimed at the heart of Germany and the destruction of her armed forces. ❞**

—Allied orders to General Eisenhower, February 12, 1944

British ports filled up with transport ships. Airfields were packed with fighters and bombers. By early June 1944, about three million Allied soldiers, sailors, and airmen were assembled for the assault.

"I'm standing on a rooftop looking out over London. At the moment, everything is quiet. For reasons of national as well as personal security, I'm unable to tell you the exact location from which I'm speaking. Off to my left, far away in the distance, I can see just that faint, red, angry snap of antiaircraft bursts against the steel-blue sky. But the guns are so far away that it's impossible to hear them from this location. About five minutes ago, the guns in the immediate vicinity were working."

Edward R. Murrow spoke these words from a London rooftop on September 22, 1940. For two weeks, the German air force had been bombing the British capital city, day and night, trying to blast Britain into surrender. Londoners huddled inside subway stations to escape the destruction on the streets above them. Murrow, a U.S. reporter for CBS radio, narrated the scene to listeners back in the United States. Murrow's courageous reporting from London helped convince many Americans that the time had come to join the Allies.

Edward R. Murrow is remembered as one of the finest reporters in U.S. history. Born in Greensboro, North Carolina, he joined CBS as a young man. The network sent him to Europe in 1937. When war came, he was there to record its sights, sounds, smells, and horrors. In addition to reporting, he supervised a corps of other CBS correspondents in Europe.

EDWARD R. MURROW walks through London, England, in the early 1940s.

Murrow continued broadcasting after the war. In 1950 he hosted a radio news show called *Hear It Now. Hear It Now* became *See It Now* and moved to television in 1952. In 1961 President John F. Kennedy picked Murrow to head the U.S. Information Agency. This organization used the media and educational programs to promote U.S. policies and positions to foreign countries. Murrow remained in the job until 1964. He died in 1965.

Eisenhower planned to drop three airborne divisions (parachutists) into Normandy and then to land five divisions on its beaches.

The attack would involve 175,000 men, 20,000 vehicles, 1,500 tanks, and 12,000 planes. "The mighty host [invasion force]," Eisenhower said, "was tense as a coiled spring . . . a great human spring, coiled for the moment when its energy should be released and it would vault the English Channel [the body of water that separates Great Britain from continental Europe] in the greatest amphibious assault ever attempted."

Such monumental invasion preparations could not be kept secret. German intelligence knew an invasion was coming. But the Allies tried to deceive the Germans about the specifics of when and where the invasion would be launched. They built an elaborate dummy headquarters at Dover, England. Allied radio operators sent fake messages, knowing the Germans would intercept them. The Allies leaked details of a fictional invasion at Calais, France, northeast of Normandy. They spread rumors of Allied attacks against German-held Holland and Norway.

The Germans were indeed confused by this information. Nevertheless, they organized coastal defenses in Normandy. They planted minefields, barbed wire, and other murderous hazards along the beaches. They flooded and booby-trapped offshore areas where parachutists might land. On the hills above the beaches, they built giant concrete fortifications called pillboxes.

■ D-DAY

General Eisenhower had chosen June 4, 1944, for the undertaking. But on that day, a near-hurricane wind was howling. Wild surf pounded the beaches of Normandy. Eisenhower postponed the invasion while he looked desperately for a hole in the storm.

The sea calmed on the night of June 5. Eisenhower decided to make his move. The great amphibious invasion force, including four thousand ships and eleven thousand airplanes, set out for the Normandy coast. "The tide has turned," Eisenhower announced. "The free men of the world are marching together to victory!"

Eisenhower sent a written message to his troops:

You are about to embark upon the Great Crusade, toward which we have striven these many months. The eyes of the world are upon you. The hopes and prayers of liberty-loving people everywhere march with you. In company with our brave Allies and brothers-in-arms on other Fronts, you will bring about the destruction of the German war machine, the elimination of Nazi tyranny over the oppressed peoples of Europe, and security for ourselves in a free world.

A little after midnight, U.S. and British paratroopers (parachutists) began jumping behind German lines. Many jumped into high winds and misty clouds. Some landed many miles from their targets. Others got caught in treetops, dangling from their parachutes. Still more, weighted down with equipment or tangled in their parachute lines, drowned in swamps. But as more and more paratroopers landed successfully, they joined together and began knocking out German guns.

GENERAL EISENHOWER speaks with paratroopers in Britain on June 6, 1944—D-day.

June 6 was D-day—the day troops hit the beaches at Normandy. As dawn broke, the Germans peered from their pillboxes. They were startled to see a vast flotilla of ships sliding out of the morning mist. That same morning, President Roosevelt spoke to U.S. citizens about the invasion via radio: "Our sons, pride of our Nation, this day have set out upon a mighty endeavor, a struggle to preserve our Republic, our religion, and our civilization and to set free a suffering humanity."

At six thirty in the morning, the first assault wave hit five beaches, which

"The free men of the world are marching together to victory!"

—General Dwight D. Eisenhower, June 5, 1944

the Allies had nicknamed Utah, Omaha, Gold, Juno, and Sword. Infantrymen (foot soldiers) approached in landing craft and then waded ashore through the water. Offshore, Allied battleships and cruisers shot at selected targets. Men unloaded tanks, jeeps, and trucks onto the beach. In the vast confusion of landing, many men died. Some drowned in deep water. Others fell to German gunfire as they waded ashore.

U.S. SOLDIERS LAND ON OMAHA BEACH during the D-day invasion in France on June 6, 1944.

Fighting was fiercest on Omaha Beach. It quickly became a smoking grave-yard of wrecked boats, drowned trucks, and burned-out tanks. Among them sprawled the bodies of the dead, the dying, and the wounded. U.S. journalist Ernie Pyle was with the invasion force on Omaha. He wrote,

> The wreckage was vast and startling. . . . For a mile [1.6 km] out from the beach there were scores of tanks and trucks and boats that were not visible, for they were at the bottom of the water—swamped by overloading, or hit by shells, or sunk by mines. Most of their crews were lost. There were trucks tipped half over and swamped, partly sunken barges, and the angled-up corners of jeeps, and small landing craft half submerged. . . . On the beach itself, high and dry, were all kinds of wrecked vehicles. There were tanks that had only just made the beach before being knocked out. There were jeeps that had burned . . . smashed bulldozers and big stacks of thrown-away life belts and piles of shells still waiting to be moved. In the water floated empty life rafts and soldiers' packs . . . and stacks of broken, rusting rifles.

At Omaha and the other beaches, the Allies rallied. Men charged forward, until unit by unit they reached the heights beyond the beaches. They knocked out enemy positions one by one. By nightfall of June 6, nearly 155,000 Allied troops were ashore and had successfully taken about 80 square miles (207 sq. km) of France. By June 27, one million Allied troops were in Normandy, ready to surge eastward across France into Germany.

■ WAR'S END

Following the D-day invasion, Adolf Hitler fought the Allies with increasing frenzy. In December 1944, his armies attacked in the Ardennes Forest in Belgium, Luxembourg, and France. In the hard-fought Battle of the Bulge, the Allies successfully stopped the German advance and continued their march toward Germany.

Hitler had declared that his empire, the Third Reich, would last one thousand years. But by early 1945, his armies were falling apart. All along the

These prisoners at the Buchenwald concentration camp in Germany were liberated by the Allies in 1945.

Rhine River in southwestern Germany, the Germans retreated. Seven Allied armies were in hot pursuit. By April 1945, General Eisenhower was 300 miles (483 km) from Berlin, the German capital. The Soviet Union, an Allied nation that included Russia, had troops just 3 miles (5 km) east of the city. By then Allied bombers had reduced Berlin to a blackened skeleton.

Despite the positive news on the war front, Americans mourned at home. Beloved president Franklin Roosevelt, by then in his fourth term, died on April 12, 1945. Vice President Harry S. Truman became the new U.S. president.

As the Allies broke through the walls of Hitler's Third Reich, they saw the full horror of Nazi atrocities. The Nazis had operated a series of concentration camps, or death camps. There, under orders from Hitler, Nazi soldiers had starved and murdered more than 10 million people, including nearly 6 million Jews. At the Buchenwald camp, the U.S. Third Army found gas chambers for killing inmates, dead bodies piled in heaps, crematories for burning bodies, and living prisoners who were little more than skeletons. As camp after camp was liberated, a cold fury filled the troops. General Eisenhower sent messages to leaders in Washington, D.C., and London. He asked journalists and U.S. and British lawmakers to come to Germany to see the atrocities firsthand.

At the start of World War II, racial segregation prevailed in the U.S. military. African American troops served in segregated (separate) units. White officers wouldn't entrust blacks with combat assignments. Instead, they assigned African American troops to menial jobs. In the army, black soldiers loaded and unloaded ships. In the navy, they served food to officers. Very few African Americans became officers.

But African American troops made some gains during World War II. In 1940 President Roosevelt promoted army colonel Benjamin O. Davis Sr. to the rank of brigadier general. Davis was the first black soldier to reach this rank. As the war went on, the U.S. Coast Guard and U.S. Navy integrated some units. African American soldiers and marines, although still in segregated units, were eventually allowed to serve in combat.

Benjamin Davis's son, Benjamin O. Davis Jr., followed his father into army service. At the Tuskegee Institute in Alabama, Davis and other black soldiers learned to fly airplanes. Davis went on to command the all-black, Tuskegee-trained 99th Pursuit Squadron, which flew missions in North Africa. Davis then commanded the Tuskegee-trained 332nd Fighter Group, which escorted bomber pilots to their missions in Europe. Many Tuskegee Airmen, as Davis and his fellow black flyers were called, earned medals for their wartime achievements. Davis earned the Distinguished Flying Cross.

Throughout World War II and afterward, African American leaders pushed for an end to segregation in the U.S. military. Success came in 1948, when President Truman signed an executive order integrating all military branches.

23

TUSKEGEE AIRMEN attend a military briefing in Italy in 1945.

At last, Germany collapsed. On the afternoon of April 30, 1945, Adolf Hitler—knowing that defeat was at hand—committed suicide with a pistol shot to the head. On May 2, Berlin fell to the Allies. On May 7, in a small schoolhouse at the city of Rheims, France, the Germans surrendered. The next day, Americans and the British celebrated VE (Victory in Europe) Day. The heads of the victorious countries made speeches, praising the warriors who had fought for freedom.

But war was still raging in the Pacific. President Truman struggled with a big decision. Should he use a nuclear bomb against Japan? This new super-weapon was tens of thousands of times more powerful than ordinary bombs. Truman knew that dropping a nuclear bomb would take many thousands of Japanese lives. But he also believed that thousands of additional U.S. troops would die if fighting in Asia continued. Ultimately, Truman decided to drop a nuclear bomb on the Japanese city of Hiroshima.

The first bomb hit Hiroshima on August 6, 1945. When the Japanese didn't surrender, three days later, a second bomb dropped on Nagasaki. The destruction was enormous. The blasts flattened both cities and engulfed them

Residents of Hiroshima, Japan, walk along its devastated streets after Allies **DESTROYED THE CITY WITH A NUCLEAR BOMB** in 1945.

in flames. At Hiroshima seventy-eight thousand people died immediately. At Nagasaki the initial death toll was more than forty thousand. (In the following months and years, an additional two hundred thousand people died an agonizing death by radiation poisoning.) One survivor described the scene in Nagasaki:

> The air flashed a brilliant yellow and there was a huge blast of wind. . . . Later, when I came to my senses, I noticed a hole had been blown in the roof, all the glass had been shattered, and that the glass had cut my shoulder and I was bleeding. When I went outside, the sky had turned from blue to black and the black rain started to fall. . . . All that I knew had disappeared. Only the concrete and iron skeletons of the buildings remained. There were dead bodies everywhere.

A few days after the bombings, Japan's emperor announced, "I cannot bear to see my innocent people suffer any longer." The Japanese surrendered to the Allies on August 14, 1945. Again, people in the United States celebrated. This time, the celebration was called VJ (Victory in Japan) Day. On September 2, Japan signed an official surrender agreement aboard the battleship *Missouri* in Tokyo Bay. World War II was over.

A sailor and an unknown woman **CELEBRATE THE SURRENDER OF JAPAN** with a kiss in Times Square, New York City, on August 15, 1945.

Conference delegates unanimously adopt the UNITED NATIONS CHARTER in San Francisco, California, on June 26, 1945. The charter established the international peacekeeping body known as the United Nations.

CHAPTER TWO

SUPERPOWER:
LEADING THE FREE WORLD

World War II killed millions of people, left millions more homeless, and devastated much of Europe and Asia. As the war was raging, many people asked: how can we prevent such destruction in the future? Some people envisioned a peacekeeping organization, with representatives from all the world's nations. This group would try to keep wars from starting and try to end any wars that did break out.

It was not a new idea. After World War I, a group of nations had formed a peacekeeping organization called the League of Nations. But, as the events of the 1930s and 1940s showed, the League had not been effective in preventing wars. (The United States had never joined the League.)

By the end of World War II, the need for a new peacekeeping organization seemed urgent. It was clear that future wars would probably involve nuclear weapons—and unspeakable destruction. British prime minister Clement Attlee explained: "I think it is well that we should make up our minds that if the world is again involved in a war on a scale compared with that from which we have just emerged, every weapon will be used. We may confidentially expect full-scale atomic [nuclear] warfare which will result in the destruction of great cities, the death of millions."

Defendants at THE NUREMBERG TRIALS in Germany listen to the proceedings under armed guard.

The actions of Nazi Germany during World War II—notably, the systematic murder of six million Jews and five million other Europeans—were unspeakably horrific. After the war, the Allies wanted to bring the perpetrators of Nazi war crimes to justice. The United States, Great Britain, the Soviet Union, and France organized a series of trials to judge Nazi leaders for their actions. The trials took place in Nuremberg, Germany, the site of many huge Nazi Party rallies before and during World War II.

Adolf Hitler and his aides Joseph Goebbels and Heinrich Himmler had all committed suicide at the end of the war. But Hermann Goering, Hitler's second in command, was still alive. He and twenty-one other Nazi leaders went on trial in Nuremberg in November 1945.

The defendants were charged with a series of war crimes, including carrying out a war of aggression, murdering prisoners of war and civilians (nonmilitary citizens), using civilians as slave labor, conducting inhumane medical experiments, and murdering people because of political beliefs, race, or religion. It took more than a day just to read the charges. All the defendants pleaded not guilty.

In a trial lasting almost a year, a panel of eight international judges heard evidence against the defendants. Nineteen of them were found guilty. Twelve, including Hermann Goering, were sentenced to death by hanging. Others received long prison sentences. Before he could be hanged, Goering committed suicide by taking poison.

After the first trial, the United States worked on its own to prosecute additional Nazi war criminals. It conducted twelve more trials at Nuremberg between 1946 and 1949. These trials involved 185 additional defendants, and 142 of them were found guilty. Some were executed, while others went to prison.

U.S. leaders agreed that the time was right for a new peacekeeping organization. Shortly before his death, Franklin Roosevelt wrote (for a speech that he never delivered), "Today we are faced with the pre-eminent fact that, if civilization is to survive we must cultivate the science of human relationships—the ability of all peoples, of all kinds, to live together and work together in the same world, at peace."

In the spring of 1945, as World War II was ending in Europe, nations from around the world sent delegates to a meeting in San Francisco, California. The delegates hammered out the structure of the new organization, called the United Nations (UN). The UN was officially established on October 24, 1945. It had fifty founding member nations. The group held meetings in London for one year before moving to new headquarters in New York City in 1946.

■ THE BALANCE OF POWER

The United States took a lead role in the United Nations. The nation was perfectly poised to lead the world into a new, more peaceful future. The United States had emerged from World War II both strong and prosperous. It had helped restore freedom to millions of people. It had proven its military might on the battlefields of Europe and the Pacific.

But its strength came not from manpower alone. It was superior U.S. technology—advanced radar, bombers, fighters, and ships—that had helped the Allies win the war. The pinnacle of this technology was the nuclear bomb. The United States was the only nation with this superweapon. And the super*weapon* made the United States a super*power*.

Another global superpower also emerged after World War II. It was the Soviet Union. During the war, the Soviets had fought alongside the

"If civilization is to survive we must cultivate the science of human relationships—the ability of all peoples, of all kinds, to live together and work together in the same world, at peace."

—*President Franklin Roosevelt, suggesting the need for the United Nations, 1945*

United States and the other Allies to defeat dictatorship in Europe. Ironically, the Soviet Union was itself a dictatorship. Led by the brutal Joseph Stalin, the Soviet Union denied its people basic rights and freedoms. It was also a Communist nation, which meant that the central government controlled all business and the economy. The government even told people where to live and where to work.

At a meeting in early 1945, as the war in Europe was winding down, Franklin Roosevelt, Joseph Stalin, and British prime minister Winston Churchill met in the Ukrainian town of Yalta. The three leaders pledged to create democratic governments in Europe once Germany was finally defeated.

The Soviet Union quickly broke the agreement. In 1945 and 1946, Soviet-

British prime minister Winston Churchill *(left)*, U.S. president Franklin D. Roosevelt *(center)*, and Soviet marshal Joseph Stalin *(right)* **MEET AT YALTA IN 1945**.

Harry S. Truman, the thirty-third president of the United States, was born in Lamar, Missouri, in 1884. In 1890 his family moved to Independence, Missouri. The young bespectacled Harry was an avid reader. He also enjoyed playing the piano. After high school, Truman held a variety of jobs. He served in the army during World War I, earning the rank of captain. In 1919 Truman married his childhood sweetheart, Elizabeth "Bess" Wallace. Also in 1919, he and a friend opened a men's clothing store in Kansas City, Missouri.

The store went broke, and Truman found a new career: politics. A Democrat, he held local offices before moving on to the U.S. Senate in 1934. In the Senate, Truman earned a reputation for honesty. When World War II broke out, he headed a committee to investigate waste and corruption in defense spending.

After much political wrangling, the Democrats nominated Truman as Franklin

HARRY S. TRUMAN in 1949

Roosevelt's running mate (vice-presidential candidate) in 1944. Roosevelt won the election—his fourth presidential victory—and Truman became vice president of the United States.

He had been in office only eight-three days when President Roosevelt died, making Truman the new president. Under his guidance the war ended in Europe in May 1945. In August Truman made the decision to drop two nuclear bombs on Japan. With World War II over, Truman turned his attention to the fight against Communism. He won a surprise victory over Thomas Dewey in the 1948 presidential election.

During his second term, he continued to fight Communism, taking the nation to war against Communist forces in North Korea in 1950. When his term ended in 1952, Truman retired from public life. He returned to Independence, where he wrote his memoirs and actively followed political events. Truman died in 1972.

backed Communists took over governments in Eastern Europe one by one. The nations became Soviet "satellites," taking their orders from the Soviet government.

The United States and Great Britain were alarmed. They had fought to save Europe from the brutal dictatorship of Adolf Hitler only to see Eastern Europe fall to another repressive regime. In March 1946, Winston Churchill warned that an "iron curtain" had descended across Europe. The curtain that he referred to was the dividing line between Communist Eastern Europe and democratic Western Europe.

■ FROM HOT WAR TO COLD WAR

Once allies, the United States and the Soviet Union quickly became enemies. Most Americans saw Communism as a repressive, unjust system of government. They watched with anger as the Soviets forced Communism on neighboring nations. The Soviets, for their part, defended the Communist philosophy. They argued that Communism was a just system in which everyone shared equally in a nation's wealth.

Historians call the conflict between the United States and the Soviet Union the Cold War (1945–1991). In this new war, U.S. and Soviet soldiers never fought one another directly. Instead, the two powerful nations built up their armed forces and weapons stockpiles. In the late 1940s, the Soviets worked furiously to develop their own nuclear bomb.

As the Soviets grabbed power in Eastern Europe, President Truman was determined to halt Soviet aggression. He vowed to contain, or hold back, the expansion of Communism throughout the world. In 1947 the Truman administration created the Central Intelligence Agency (CIA). This spy organization was designed to gather information about foreign governments—especially the Soviet and other Communist governments. Also in 1947, the United States helped Greece and Turkey defeat Communist takeovers. But the Communist advance was not so easily stopped. The Soviet Union set up a Communist state in North Korea in 1948. Communists took over China in 1949.

Hoping to strengthen its defenses against the Soviets, the United States joined with ten Western European nations in April 1949. They created a military alliance called the North Atlantic Treaty Organization (NATO).

NATO's goal was to prevent further Soviet expansion in Europe. The Cold War was growing more and more heated.

On August 29, 1949, the Soviet Union tested its first nuclear bomb. The United States was shocked. If the Soviets also had "the bomb," then Americans had lost the upper hand in the Cold War. A U.S. military document explained, "The United States has lost its capability of making an effective atomic attack upon the war-making potential of the USSR [Soviet Union] without danger of retaliation in kind." So if the United States attacked the Soviets with nuclear weapons, it could expect a nuclear attack in return. For both nations, the next step was to create bigger, deadlier bombs—and more bombs than the enemy had.

Following World War II, Germany was divided into four zones. Berlin, the capital, was completely within the Soviet zone but was also divided. The Communist Soviets tried to stop supplies from reaching the other non-communist sections of the city. To combat this, the U.S. flew in food and fuel to West Berlin *(below)*. This was known as **THE BERLIN AIRLIFT** and was one of the first confrontations of the Cold War.

FIRST CARGO OF
CARIBBEAN SUGAR
SHIPPED UNDER MARSHALL
AID

Officials watch the first food supplies being loaded onto a ship bound for Europe under **THE MARSHALL PLAN**.

1940s

34

AMERICA IN THE

After World War II, Europe lay in ruins. The economy was devastated. In big cities, many factories, warehouses, and other buildings were bombed-out shells. In the countryside, farmers' fields were covered with tank tracks and shell craters. Millions of Europeans were homeless and hungry.

To help Europeans get back on their feet, the U.S. Congress passed the European Recovery Act of 1948. The act was nicknamed the Marshall Plan because U.S. secretary of state George C. Marshall had first suggested it. Under the plan, the United States sent more than $12 billion in food, machinery, fuel, and other goods to Western Europe over a four-year span. (The United States had offered to help all the nations of Europe. But by 1948, the Cold War had begun. The Soviet satellite nations of Eastern Europe rejected U.S. aid.)

The Marshall Plan not only provided Western European nations with badly needed food and other goods, it also strengthened them politically. As their economies recovered, the nations of Western Europe set up democratic governments. They joined with the United States to create NATO as a defense against the Soviet Union.

■ "ARE YOU NOW OR HAVE YOU EVER BEEN . . . ?"

As the Cold War got hotter, a kind of anti-Communist fever gripped the United States. Many Americans wondered: Were Communist agents living in the United States? What if Soviet spies were lurking among them, planning to overthrow the U.S. government?

These questions were not so far-fetched. In fact, some Americans *were* Communists. Many were members of the American Communist Party. Others had once been party members but had quit the party after learning about Joseph Stalin's brutal form of Communism in the Soviet Union. Still others had no connections to Communist organizations but were nevertheless interested in Communist theory. Many backed the Communist philosophy that everyone should share equally in society's riches. For many years in the early and mid-twentieth century, Americans freely explored Communism just as they did many other ideas.

COMMUNISTS ATTEND A RALLY at Madison Square Garden in New York City in 1946.

But once the Cold War began, it was no longer acceptable for Americans to have Communist leanings. U.S. leaders said that anyone with Communist connections was automatically disloyal to the United States. In 1947 President Truman established loyalty boards. These agencies investigated federal government workers. Those with Communist ties lost their jobs. Even people who weren't Communists sometimes got in trouble. Sometimes the government fired people simply for having left-wing or radical political views.

The U.S. government ramped up its hunt for Communists in the United States. The House Un-American Activities Committee (HUAC), a committee of the U.S. Congress, began to investigate individuals and groups suspected of disloyalty to the United States. Some lawmakers thought that Hollywood, with its many artists, writers, and freethinkers, was a hotbed of Communism. In 1947 HUAC began to summon actors, directors, producers, and screenwriters to testify about their Communist connections. "Are you now or have you

Members of the **HOUSE UN-AMERICAN ACTIVITIES COMMITTEE** convene in Washington, D.C., in 1948. Committee member Richard Nixon—future president of the United States—is seated at the far left.

ever been a member of the Communist Party?" the investigators asked witnesses. People who admitted to Communist ties lost their jobs. Those who refused to testify went to jail for contempt of Congress.

" Are you now or have you ever been a member of the Communist Party? "

—House Un-American Activities Committee, question posed to suspected Communists, 1940s and 1950s

That was just the beginning. Soon Hollywood studio heads also started hunting for Communists. The studios blacklisted, or refused to hire, actors, writers, and other film professionals with Communist ties—or those simply suspected of having them. Careers went down the drain. The famous playwright and screenwriter Lillian Hellman was blacklisted in 1949. She didn't work in Hollywood again until 1966.

The attack on Communism in the United States was called the Red Scare, because red was the color associated with Communism and the Soviet Union. Although HUAC actually did find a few Communist spies, most of its targets were innocent of any wrongdoing. What's more, the investigators often violated suspects' constitutional rights, such as the right to a fair trial, freedom of speech, and freedom of assembly. As the 1940s came to a close, the Red Scare was just getting started. It would reach new levels of hysteria in the 1950s.

THE FIRST ATOMIC BOMB explodes over the New Mexico
desert on July 16, 1945.

CHAPTER THREE

THE ATOMIC AGE:
SCIENCE AND TECHNOLOGY

In April 1943, dozens of top physicists made their way to the remote mountain town of Los Alamos, New Mexico. When they arrived, they saw that workers were busy building apartments, offices, and laboratories. The physicists didn't know why they were there. All they knew was that fellow physicist Robert Oppenheimer had recruited them for a secret government project. Finally, team leader Robert Serber gave the physicists their assignment: "to produce a practical military weapon in the form of a bomb in which energy is released by a fast neutron chain reaction in one or more of the materials known to show nuclear fission."

The scientists were startled. They had been brought to Los Alamos to build a nuclear bomb—something that no one had ever done before. The weapon would be thousands of times more powerful—and more deadly—than a conventional bomb. Just 2.2 pounds (1 kg) of nuclear fuel (about the size of a golf ball) could release as much energy as 20,000 tons (18,144 metric tons) of the explosive TNT. A nuclear bomb would be a superweapon that would win World War II for the Allies.

Most of the scientists didn't know that the United States had been working on the project for several years. Early in the war, the U.S. government had learned that German scientists were trying to build a nuclear bomb of their own. The United States wanted to build a bomb before the Germans did. The government recruited the best minds in science. Many of them were Europeans who had escaped to the United States when dictators came to power in Germany and Italy in the 1930s. Even world-famous German Jewish physicist Albert Einstein assisted the Americans.

Research began at several U.S. universities. At Oak Ridge, Tennessee, and Hanford, Washington, the government built plants for manufacturing the necessary nuclear materials. The bomb itself would be built at Los Alamos. The program was run by the U.S. Army Corps of Engineers. It was code-named the Manhattan Project because it was originally headquartered in Manhattan in New York City.

At its peak, the Manhattan Project employed 130,000 people. At the three work sites, military police patrolled the grounds. Workers had to pass through tall gates and guard towers to get to their jobs. To prevent secrets from leaking out, the army read employees' mail. Some workers constructed giant laboratories and factory buildings. Others operated machines and monitored gauges. Workers learned only how to do their jobs—and knew nothing else about the project. Only a few people knew what they were helping to build.

Workers leave the **OAK RIDGE NUCLEAR FACILITY IN TENNESSEE**. Many Americans worked toward the development of the atomic bomb—whether they knew it at the time or not.

When U.S. Army general Leslie Groves wanted to find a physicist to head the Manhattan Project, he wanted the world's best—and the best was J. Robert Oppenheimer. "He's a genius. A real genius," Groves said about Oppenheimer. The son of wealthy New Yorkers, Oppenheimer had studied at Boston's Harvard University as an undergraduate. By the time he received his PhD in physics from Gottingen University in Germany, he had a reputation as one of the brightest minds in physics.

In the 1930s, Oppenheimer taught physics at the University of California at Berkeley and at the California Institute of Technology in Pasadena. He also awakened to political and economic injustice during those years. To address these issues, he joined a number of political organizations with ties to the Communist Party. In 1941, before the Manhattan Project officially began, Oppenheimer joined other physicists in studying uranium-235, one of the ingredients in nuclear bomb making. In 1943 General Groves chose Oppenheimer to head the bomb-building work at Los Alamos.

After the bombing of Hiroshima and Nagasaki, Oppenheimer felt uneasy about a future with nuclear weapons. As an adviser to the U.S. Atomic Energy Commission and the Department of Defense, he argued for international controls on atomic weapons and atomic energy. In 1953 Oppenheimer argued against construction of hydrogen

OPPENHEIMER stands in the New Mexico desert, where the atomic bomb was first tested, in 1945.

bombs, which are many times more powerful and destructive than nuclear bombs. His opposition to these weapons won him many enemies in the military and federal government.

By the 1950s, the Red Scare was in full swing. Investigators began looking into Oppenheimer's past and discovered his Communist connections from the 1930s. He was branded a Communist and barred from government work. The incident damaged his reputation and his career. He withdrew from public life, heading the Institute for Advanced Study at New Jersey's Princeton University until his death in 1967.

41

In July 1945, the atomic bomb was ready for testing. Project leaders chose a valley in the desert of southern New Mexico—a place called the Jornada del Muerto (Journey of Death)—for the test site. The test was code-named Trinity.

At five thirty in the morning on July 16, a physicist activated the bomb by remote control. Seconds later, a giant white light filled the sky. A gigantic fireball rose above the desert. Scientists standing more than 10 miles (16 km) away felt a pulse of heat and winds of hurricane force. They heard a deafening roar. Light from the explosion was visible 180 miles (290 km) away.

One scientist described the explosion: "It was a sunrise such as the world had never seen, a great green super sun climbing in a fraction of a second to a height of more than eight thousand feet [2,440 meters], rising ever higher until it touched the clouds. . . . It was as if the earth had opened and the skies had split." Another physicist shouted, "The sun can't hold a candle to it."

Chief physicist J. Robert Oppenheimer offered this assessment: "A few people laughed, a few people cried, most people were silent. There floated through my mind a line from the 'Bhagavad-Gita' [a sacred Hindu text] in which Krishna [a Hindu god] is trying to persuade the Prince that he should do his duty: 'I am become death: the destroyer of worlds.'"

Workers attach the world's **FIRST ATOMIC BOMB** to a test tower before detonation in New Mexico in July 1945.

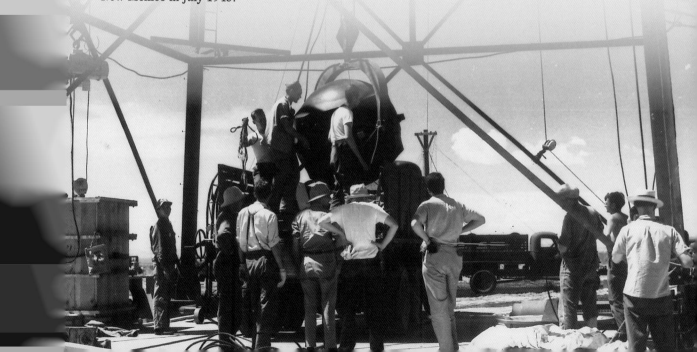

> **"It was a sunrise such as the world had never seen, a great green super sun climbing in a fraction of a second to a height of more than eight thousand feet [2,440 m], rising ever higher until it touched the clouds."**

—Manhattan Project scientist, describing the explosion of the first atomic bomb, July 16, 1945

The test was a success—and many Americans were eager to use atomic bombs against the enemy. By July 1945, the war in Europe was over. Japan was being badly beaten, but it refused to surrender. Military commanders felt it was time to use the new superweapon that they had worked so hard on and spent more than $2 billion to create.

President Truman agreed. Although Oppenheimer and other physicists warned that nuclear warfare could potentially destroy the human race, U.S. commanders were determined to move ahead. The atomic bombs did their jobs as planned. Dropped on Hiroshima on August 6 and Nagasaki on August 9, two nuclear bombs devastated the cities and led to a Japanese surrender on August 14, 1945.

■ A DECADE OF LIFE AND DEATH

Throughout history, some of the most noteworthy scientific advances have resulted from warfare. That's because nations employ their brightest scientists to create new weapons, military vehicles, and other equipment during wartime. The most famous example from World War II was the nuclear bomb.

Scientists also created advanced radar during World War II. Radar is an electronic system that sends out radio waves. The waves bounce off objects and return to the sender. The returning waves show the objects' location. When World War II began, radar was very basic. The British built radar stations along the shoreline to detect enemy planes and ships. The Germans used radar systems too. After the United States entered the war, U.S. and British scientists worked together to make radar more precise and more effective. They developed mobile radar systems for individual planes and boats. The British and Americans also developed techniques to interfere with the enemy's radar systems.

Engineers also improved sonar during World War II. Sonar is similar to radar, only it uses sound waves instead of radio waves. Sonar helped the Allies detect underwater objects, such as enemy mines and submarines. U.S. engineers also designed more powerful and accurate artillery, faster and lighter planes, sturdier ships, and more efficient tanks during World War II.

Medicine took great leaps during World War II. By then doctors knew about penicillin, a lifesaving antibiotic, but they didn't know how to produce it in large quantities. That changed early in the war, when Pfizer, a U.S. pharmaceutical company, began large-scale production of penicillin. On the battlefields of Europe and the Pacific, penicillin saved countless lives.

Military doctors desperately needed blood to transfuse into wounded soldiers. But even when refrigerated, whole blood spoils quickly. At military and battlefield hospitals, supplies were constantly going bad. Around 1940, Charles Drew, a Washington, D.C.–based doctor, solved this problem by separating blood into two parts—blood plasma and blood cells. The separated parts could be frozen or dried and then shipped overseas. Separated blood lasts much longer than refrigerated whole blood. Early in the war, Drew organized the Blood for Britain program—a U.S. blood donation program. The American Red Cross also set up blood banks, where people could donate blood for storage and shipment overseas.

By the end of 1943, Americans were donating 100,000 pints (47,320 liters) of blood per week. But in the racially segregated U.S. military, even blood was segregated. Medical staff wouldn't infuse white soldiers with blood from black donors or black soldiers with blood

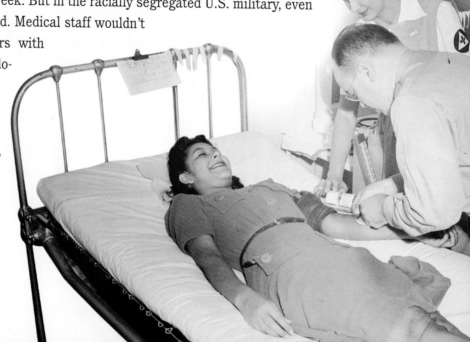

A WOMAN DONATES BLOOD at a Red Cross donor center during the war.

from white donors. Interestingly, Charles Drew—the man who pioneered blood banking—was an African American.

The medical advances of the 1940s saved millions of lives. But it wasn't just soldiers who benefited. The large-scale production of penicillin and the separation and storage of blood also saved civilian lives. In 1943 a medical researcher named Selman Waksman discovered a new antibiotic, streptomycin. Doctors used it to treat and cure tuberculosis, a previously dreaded disease. Doctors also began routinely using the Pap smear in the 1940s. The test detects cervical cancer in women. It was named for a Greek American physician, George Papanicolaou.

■ PEACETIME PRODUCTS

Post–World War II Americans enjoyed a host of new products. Some of them had been developed for soldiers on the battlefield. Manufacturers quickly realized that civilians would want them too. For instance, General Foods made dried "instant" coffee for soldiers in the field. After the war, General Foods kept selling the coffee under the brand name Maxwell House. Frozen orange juice and frozen fried potatoes were other products developed for U.S. troops and popular with U.S. consumers after the war.

Other new foods of the 1940s included M&M chocolate candies, Cheerios cereal, Reddi-wip whipping cream (the first food product in an aerosol spray can), V-8 vegetable juice, and boxed cake mixes. Consumers could also buy new products for food storage: Tupperware resealable containers and Reynolds Wrap aluminum foil.

Dow Chemical Company invented Styrofoam in 1942. It was first used to make life rafts for the U.S. Coast Guard. After the war, people found dozens of uses for Styrofoam: as insulation, protective packaging, and crafts material.

Eastman Kodak introduced color film (called Kodacolor) to consumers in 1942. Polaroid introduced its Land Camera in 1948. This remarkable invention was a camera and a darkroom in one. After you snapped the picture, the camera developed the film and produced a finished photographic print. The whole process took just sixty seconds.

Other new products of the 1940s included the clock radio, the car air conditioner, and the car seat belt (optional on Nash automobiles, it fit over the laps

A boy plays with a **SLINKY**. While experimenting with springs, naval engineer Richard James created the toy during World War II.

by train. Many families owned cars, but gas was in limited supply, since the nation was saving gas for military vehicles. Limiting travel further, automakers stopped producing passenger cars in 1942 (switching instead to building military vehicles) and didn't start again until 1945. Even with wartime restrictions, Americans had many transportation options. In addition to trains, people commonly traveled on streetcars, buses, and subways. Servicemen traveled overseas in ships.

Before the 1940s, people used airplanes for military missions, delivering mail and cargo, exploration, and adventure. But other than pilots, few civilians traveled by airplane. At that time, planes could not fly very far or very fast. At high altitudes, where air pressure is low, it was difficult for airplane passengers to breathe. Air travel began to improve in the 1940s. Engineers devised pressurized cabins, which allowed passengers to breathe normally during high-altitude flight. The first pressurized commercial flight took off from New York City on July 8, 1940. After a stop in Kansas City,

of front-seat passengers only). For children, Slinky, Silly Putty, Scrabble, and Lego were the new toys and games of the 1940s.

◼ GET UP AND GO

The 1940s was a decade of mobility. Jobs were plentiful in defense plants, located mainly in big cities. Many civilians moved to distant cities to take the jobs. Soldiers moved to bases across the United States for training and then shipped out to battlefields overseas. Vehicles—airplanes, tanks, jeeps, and boats—were just as important to the war effort as guns and bullets.

When the decade began, Americans usually traveled long distances

—*United Airlines ad, 1947*

Missouri, the plane reached Los Angeles, California—twelve hours and eighteen minutes after leaving New York. The age of passenger flight had begun. Most airplanes of this era were equipped with sleeping berths for overnight travel.

Throughout the decade, planes got bigger and faster. They could fly at high altitudes—above clouds and storms. Still, most Americans didn't travel by airplane in the 1940s. For one thing, air travel was expensive. In 1946 TWA began flying commercial passengers from New York City across the Atlantic Ocean to Paris, France. The flight took about twenty hours and cost $675 round-trip. The average U.S. worker earned only about $2,500 a year at the time—so passenger flights were mainly for the wealthy in the 1940s.

Like passenger planes, military planes got faster and more powerful during the 1940s. The helicopter was a new invention during World War II. The military didn't use helicopters extensively, although the U.S. Coast Guard used them to carry gear and to rescue people at sea. After the war, engineers improved helicopters greatly—preparing to use them in future conflicts.

A number of other aviation firsts occurred in the 1940s. Most famously, in 1947 Chuck Yeager, a former U.S. military fighter pilot, was the first person to fly faster than the speed of sound.

47

PASSENGERS BOARD THE *FLYING CLOUD* IN 1949. It was one of the first planes to fly regularly between New York and London.

GRACE HOPPER was a 1940s computer pioneer.

ike television, computers were brand-new technology in the 1940s. The people who built and programmed computers during that decade were pioneers. One of them was Grace M. Hopper.

Hopper was born in 1906 in New York City. She attended Vassar University in Poughkeepsie, New York, and graduated with a degree in mathematics and physics. She then took a job teaching mathematics at Vassar. At the same time, she attended Yale University in Connecticut, where she earned a master's degree and a PhD in mathematics.

In 1943 Hopper joined the Waves, the women's branch of the U.S. Navy. The navy assigned her to a project at Harvard University. There, she and other experts worked with one of the world's first computers. It was called the Mark I.

Computers of the 1940s were nothing like modern computers. The Mark I was a series of large devices that together took up an entire room. Altogether, the machines weighed 5 tons (4.5 metric tons), had 760,000 separate parts, and contained 500 miles (804 km) of electrical wiring. It took four seconds for the Mark I to perform a simple multiplication problem. But at the time, the Mark I (and its successor the Mark II) was advanced technology.

One day in 1945, Hopper was working on the Mark II when a moth got trapped in the machine, mucking up the works. For many years, technicians had been using the term *bug* to describe a problem with electronic equipment. The moth in Mark II was the first case of a *real* bug interfering with a computer. After that, the terms *bug* and *debugging* became common in computer lingo.

In 1949 Hopper joined the Eckert Mauchly Corporation, an early computer firm. She continued to work for the military, universities, and other businesses as a consultant and lecturer. One of Hopper's biggest contributions to computing was inventing a compiler, a program that translated English-language instructions into instructions for a computer. She also led the effort to develop COBOL, an important computer language. Hopper died in 1992.

PILOT CHUCK YEAGER stands next to his Bell X-1 rocket plane. He used it to break the sound barrier on October 14, 1947.

He traveled in the Bell X-1 rocket plane and reached a speed of more than 700 miles (1,126 km) per hour. In 1949 the U.S. plane *Lucky Lady II* was the first airplane to fly around the world nonstop. The plane refueled in midair by means of a hose connected to a fuel plane. It took ninety-four hours to make the trip.

■ A WINDOW ONTO THE FUTURE

Radio was wildly popular in the 1940s. Americans listened to radio dramas, news reports, music, and sporting events coming from cabinet-sized radios in their living rooms. President Franklin Roosevelt regularly spoke to Americans by radio. He called his speeches fireside chats. Most middle-class Americans had a radio at home—and it was by radio that Americans learned about critical world events, such as the 1941 attack on Pearl Harbor.

Television was a new and experimental invention in the 1940s. It's likely that most Americans had never even heard of television when NBC and CBS started broadcasting cartoons, sports, news, and other programs out of New York City in 1941. Only a few hundred households owned televisions—so almost all Americans missed the shows.

When the United States entered World War II, television broadcasting ended. Broadcasters devoted themselves to covering the war by radio. Companies that had been working on TV technology focused instead on creating communications equipment for the military. When the war ended, broadcasters returned to developing television.

Television programming was limited to just a few shows a day. At first, telecasts reached only cities on the East Coast. But Americans were intrigued. As more and more TV programs came on the air, more and more Americans wanted to watch them. By the end of 1949, about four million U.S. homes had TV sets. In the following decade, that number would explode.

THE WAR INCREASED THE NEED FOR MANUFACTURING and jolted the economy out of the Depression. Many women joined the workforce at this time.

CHAPTER FOUR

BUST TO BOOM:
THE 1940s ECONOMY

When the 1940s began, the U.S. economy was still in a depression. More than 8 million Americans were unemployed. People worried that "we shall never have good times again" and that Americans were "permanently licked."

Then came World War II. Almost overnight, the U.S. economy went into overdrive. The military needed ships, tanks, guns, planes, and ammunition. Soldiers needed food, medicine, and uniforms. To meet that demand, U.S. factories operated twenty-four hours a day. All at once, good-paying jobs were plentiful. Americans no longer needed government relief. One by one, the federal government shut down New Deal programs. The Depression was finally over.

■ WARTIME ECONOMICS

The entire home front was focused on the war effort—producing military materials and getting them quickly to the fighting forces. That effort took oversight and planning. The job fell to a new government agency, the War Production Board (WPB), established in January 1942. The WPB made rules and regulations about how businesses would operate. It decided which factories would produce which weapons and how many. It decided how many and which civilian products could be made. It directed scarce materials such as metal, paper, and rubber to the factories that needed them.

51

Other government agencies also helped regulate the wartime economy. The National War Labor Board negotiated disputes between defense workers and employers. Negotiations were especially important because if workers went on strike (refused to work), factories couldn't produce vital war materials. The Office of Price Administration (OPA) set prices for consumer goods and tried to limit inflation, or rising prices.

With guidance from the WPB, factories converted to wartime production. In Detroit, Michigan, the big automakers stopped making passenger cars and started building giant, four-engine B-24 bombers and other military vehicles. One typewriter factory began making machine guns. Another factory switched from making pots and pans to manufacturing steel helmets. A maker of rubber boots started producing rubber life rafts for the navy.

To keep up with the demand for wartime materials, factories employed three shifts of workers: 8:00 A.M. to 4:00 P.M., 4:00 P.M. to midnight, and midnight to 8:00 A.M. Using assembly-line techniques, factories produced goods at an astounding pace. At the Willys-Overland factory in Toledo, Ohio, rugged army jeeps rolled off the assembly line at the incredible rate of one jeep every two minutes. By the end of 1943, the United States had manufactured twice as many weapons as Germany, Italy, and Japan combined.

THIS CHRYSLER PLANT, which normally made passenger cars, switched to making tanks during the war.

U.S. productivity in World War II owed a lot to the ambition and ingenuity of industrialist Henry J. Kaiser. Kaiser was born in 1882 in upstate New York. He started work early, quitting school and taking his first job at the age of thirteen.

At the age of twenty-four, he moved to the Pacific Northwest, where he started a road-building company. Kaiser's business grew and grew. He expanded into construction, sand and gravel processing, and

HENRY J. KAISER in the early 1940s

cement production. During the 1930s, Kaiser's company helped build dams, levies, and bridges.

When World War II arrived, Kaiser applied his construction know-how to shipbuilding. He opened a string of shipyards along the Pacific Coast. There, Kaiser's workers used assembly-line techniques to build giant cargo ships called Liberty ships. Initially, it took about 230 days to build one Liberty ship. Kaiser streamlined the process, eventually knocking construction time down to just forty days. With his "get it done" spirit, Kaiser became something of a folk hero to Americans during World War II.

After the war, he embarked into new business areas: auto manufacturing, health care, housing, aviation, and steel. Henry Kaiser died in 1967. Many modern-day companies still bear his name.

Employees work on a LIBERTY SHIP AT A KAISER SHIPYARD in 1942.

THREE WOMEN work on a B-17F bomber at a plant in California in 1942.

■ HELP WANTED: WHITE, BLACK, MALE, FEMALE

As American factories geared up for war, men went off to serve in the military. Over the course of World War II, more than six million men volunteered for service. The U.S. government drafted millions more. Businesses quickly found themselves shorthanded. One young woman remembered, "Gradually everyone started going off. All the boys were graduating and instead of going on to college were taken into the army.... Pratt & Whitney [a factory]...were desperate for people to work."

Short on staff, businesses hired women for jobs that had previously been held only by men. They even hired teenagers. Wartime wages were high. In 1940 the typical white male took home $1,064 per year in pay. That figure had increased to $2,600 per year by 1944.

Jobs were plentiful, but employers were far from color blind during the war years. Early in the war, most defense plants refused to hire black workers. A. Philip Randolph, president of an African American labor union called the Brotherhood of Sleeping Car Porters, threatened a massive march on Washington, D.C., to protest this discrimination. In response, President Roosevelt issued an executive order banning racial discrimination in the defense industries. He set up the Fair Employment Practices Committee to enforce the ban.

Desperate for workers, most employers gradually complied with the president's order. They opened jobs in factories and shipyards to African Americans. Hundreds of thousands of African Americans left rural areas, especially the South, to take defense jobs in big cities. Before the war, most black women had access to just one kind of job: domestic service—that is, cooking, cleaning, and providing child care for white families. During the war, factories hired black women as well as black men. Because of the labor shortage, employers also hired African Americans as office workers, sales clerks, streetcar drivers, and other positions that had previously been reserved for whites only.

But racial discrimination did not disappear. Many white workers resented working alongside blacks and often harassed their African American coworkers. At defense plants, African Americans rarely got promotions or held management positions. Their pay was much lower than that of their white counterparts (women

> **" By 1944 . . . it was eight hours a day on Saturdays and Sundays and ten to twelve hours a day all during the week. We didn't have a day off. . . . The take-home pay was tremendous."**
>
> —*George Peabody, an employee of the Lockheed Aircraft Company, reflecting on wartime employment, n.d.*

were also paid far less than men for the same work). In most cities, African American workers crowded into run-down slums near defense plants. In several cities, racial tensions simmered and then erupted into rioting and violence between African American and white mobs.

■ STAMPS, POINTS, AND STICKERS

Waging war requires materials—food for soldiers; fabric for parachutes and uniforms; metal for guns, airplanes, and tanks; gasoline to fuel the vehicles; and rubber for tires and life rafts. To conserve these materials for the military, the government rationed (limited sales of) certain items to civilians.

The OPA was in charge of rationing. The agency distributed ration books to every U.S. family. Each book had a thin cardboard cover, with pages of tiny red and blue stamps inside. Shoppers presented the stamps when buying rationed food at the grocery store. (The bigger the family, the more stamps it got.)

To buy meat or dairy products, a shopper had to give the grocer a certain number of red stamps. For processed foods such as ketchup, the shopper had to hand over a number of blue stamps. The stamp requirements varied, depending on which foods were in short supply. The OPA issued new ration books every month or so. If a family used its stamps too quickly, it couldn't buy any rationed foods until the next book arrived.

Because of food rationing, many families grew their own. They planted backyard "victory gardens." Crops included beans, lettuce, peas, tomatoes, and radishes. Many homemakers canned and preserved their own fruit and vegetables. Sugar was rationed to 8 ounces (227 grams) per person per week, so housewives experimented with sugarless desserts. "Victory cookbooks" had recipes for sugar-free dishes and meatless meals.

Coffee was limited to 1 pound (0.5 kg) per person every five weeks. Some coffee drinkers added stretchers such as chicory and cracked wheat to their ground coffee. Others rebrewed used grounds. The resulting brew was weak. Some unhappy coffee lovers dubbed it Roosevelt Coffee.

A BOY USES A RATION BOOK to get groceries for his family during the war.

A father and his sons tend a **VICTORY GARDEN** in New York in 1944.

On December 1, 1942, nationwide gasoline rationing went into effect. Each car owner got a sticker marked with a letter of the alphabet. A driver with an A sticker received the smallest gas allotment, usually 3 gallons (11 liters) a week. B and C stickers entitled drivers to greater amounts of gas. They went to those whose driving was considered essential to the war effort, such as defense workers, farmers, and doctors. Truckers transporting food, military equipment, and other essential goods got T stickers. They could buy as much gas as needed.

Most Americans came to accept rationing, shortages, and long lines at the grocery store. Still, many people complained. Some people cheated. They stole or forged ration stamps. Some grocers quietly sold goods without taking the required stamps—but at greatly inflated prices. But most Americans followed the rules. They considered it unpatriotic to buy goods through the black (illegal) market.

■ PAYING FOR WAR

How did the U.S. government pay for all the tanks, planes, and guns that it bought from defense industries? The government got some of the money by taxing citizens and businesses. It got the rest by borrowing from banks, businesses, and individuals.

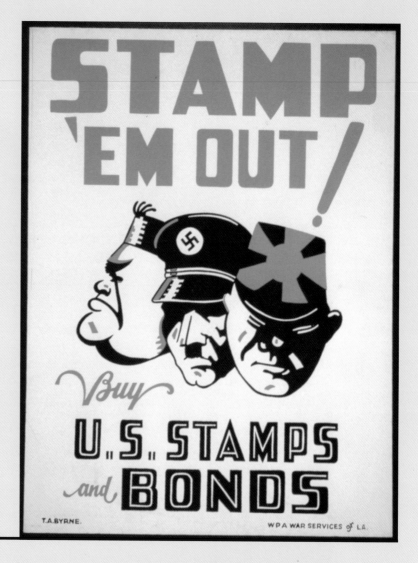

STAMP 'EM OUT!

Buy

U."S." STAMPS *and* **BONDS**

T.A.BYRNE.

WPA WAR SERVICES of LA.

Depicting the leaders of Italy, Germany, and Japan, **THIS GOVERNMENT POSTER ENCOURAGED AMERICANS TO BUY WAR BONDS.**

War bonds were one tool the government used to borrow money. The bonds were essentially loans that people made to the government. A buyer could purchase a bond for as little as $18.75. The government promised to pay back that money ten years later with interest—for a total payment of $25.

Americans eagerly helped the war effort by buying bonds. Many Hollywood stars pitched in by singing, dancing, and telling jokes at war bond drives. At one bond drive, anyone who bought $25,000 in war bonds got a kiss from movie star Hedy Lamarr. Over the course of the war, Americans purchased $135 billion in war bonds, at prices ranging from $18.75 to $10,000 apiece.

In schools, students bought "war stamps" for a dime or a quarter. Then they pooled their stamps, pasting them into albums. When full, one album of war stamps was worth an $18.75 bond. One student wrote about his experience:

The school set a goal. They were selling stamps. Each kid would buy stamps. . . . We were using our allowances and paper drives and whatever way we could to get money to purchase the stamps. . . . The goal of the school . . . was seventy-nine-to eighty-thousand dollars . . . this would be sufficient money to purchase a P-38 fighter plane. We reached the goal . . . after eight or nine months of work . . . and there was a P-38 named after the school. . . . We received a letter of commendation from some general for the school. There were pictures taken with a couple of air force men who were pilots dressed in their uniforms . . . so it was a thrill.

Actress Carole Lombard encourages Americans to buy **WAR BONDS** at a rally in 1942.

	1940s	2000s (first decade)
Average U.S. worker's income	$2,364	$35,000

TYPICAL PRICES

	1940s	2000s
Bottle of pop	5¢	$1.39
Quart of milk	17¢	$1.79
Box of cereal	27¢	$3.99
Movie ticket	40¢	$9.00
Restaurant lunch	50¢	$8.95
Man's haircut	50¢	$30.00
Man's shoes	$6.00	$79.99
Child's bicycle	$29.50	$139.99
Washing machine	$79.95	$809.99
Television	$189.95	$329.99
Four-door passenger car	$1,500	$22,000
Three-bedroom house	$5,700	$300,000

(Prices are samples only. At any given time, prices vary by year, location, size, brand, and model.)

1940s

60

AMERICA IN THE

■ HAPPY DAYS *ARE* HERE AGAIN

In 1944 and 1945, large numbers of servicemen started coming home from Europe and the Pacific. After ticker tape parades and joyful reunions with their families, they began the readjustment to civilian life. To aid in that transition, the U.S. government passed the Servicemen's Readjustment Act of 1944. The act was nicknamed the GI Bill of Rights. The bill offered soldiers unemployment pay, low-interest loans to buy houses and businesses, and money for college or job training.

Congress passed the GI Bill in part to thank soldiers for their service in World War II. But mostly, government leaders were worried about future unemployment and economic disaster. Leaders feared that if returning soldiers didn't have financial opportunities, the country would fall into another depression.

The GI Bill was a remarkable boon to returning soldiers. In vast numbers, they took advantage of its provisions for home loans and education. Very few soldiers needed to collect government unemployment pay after the war. The economy boomed in wartime and stayed robust afterward. For returning GIs, jobs and business opportunities were plentiful. Less than 20 percent of the money the government had set aside for unemployment pay was used.

At war's end, rationing also ended. Industry switched back to peacetime production. Once again, passenger cars and household goods rolled off assembly lines. Builders constructed millions of homes for returning GIs and their families. Some factories that had made airplanes, ships, and bombs during the war kept building them—this time to defend the United States against its one-time ally and newest enemy, the Soviet Union. Other companies turned their energies to new medical, household, and transportation technology. Corporations, universities, and the U.S. Treasury were all flush with cash.

The postwar U.S. economy was a success story like none other. Between 1940 and 1950, the nation's gross domestic product (GDP), the measure of all goods and services produced in the nation in one year, nearly tripled. It went from $101 billion in 1940 to almost $300 billion in 1950. Happy times had indeed arrived and at last seemed here to stay.

U.S. SOLDIERS RETURN HOME to their waiting families and friends at the end of the war.

SERVING

OUR COUNTRY

The two stars in this woman's window signal that she has TWO SONS SERVING IN THE MILITARY. Her granddaughter sits in her lap.

CHAPTER FIVE

HOME FIRES:
CIVILIAN LIFE

The attack on Pearl Harbor unified Americans into a cohesive fighting force—not only in the military but also on the home front. "We are now in this war," President Roosevelt declared in a radio address on December 9, 1941. "We are all in it—all the way. Every single man, woman, and child is a partner in the most tremendous undertaking of our American history."

"Remember Pearl Harbor" became the nation's battle cry. Most Americans were happy to do whatever they could for the war effort. They were eager to tackle unfamiliar jobs in shipyards and defense plants. After the desperate years of the 1930s, many people were also relieved to be back at work full-time.

Physically, the U.S. home front suffered little during the war years. The Axis did not bomb U.S. cities or kill civilians. But the war took a great emotional toll. Most Americans had at least one relative serving in the military. Families feared daily for their loved ones' lives. Households with a man in uniform posted a blue star in the window. If the soldier was killed, the family replaced the blue star with a gold one.

Many young couples rushed to get married before the male partner shipped overseas. For some, the decision to marry was romantic. For others, the decision was more practical. The government gave soldiers' wives a regular cash payment while their husbands were at war. And if the husband died in battle, his wife could collect on a life insurance policy. Before men left for the war, many couples conceived children. In some sad cases, fathers died in battle without ever meeting their new babies.

■ CIVIL DEFENSE

Following the attack on Pearl Harbor, Americans feared further attacks.

63

People in West Coast cities worried about additional Japanese bombings. Those on the East Coast feared the Germans. In small towns and big cities, Americans created civil defense systems, staffed in many cases by volunteers. Some workers served as air-raid wardens, who hustled their neighbors into shelters when an air-raid siren sounded. Others worked as firefighters, ambulance drivers, and nurses. One young woman, only fourteen at the time, worked as a plane spotter. Her job was to watch for enemy airplanes on the Gulf of Mexico. She remembers:

> The plane-spotter station, which looked like a fire-watching station, was built right up on the Gulf. We had a special assigned time . . . for two or three hours. . . . We were given charts and taught the shapes and silhouettes [outlines] of the planes, and we were supposed to tell how many miles away they were. It was terribly confusing in the beginning. At first, we were lucky to distinguish between an airplane and a seagull. But eventually we could identify every plane we saw. We learned to estimate distances and direction. . . . As soon as we saw a plane, we instantly reported the type and direction.

Many cities imposed nighttime blackouts, especially right after Pearl Harbor. During a blackout, people turned off streetlamps and house lights. They didn't light cigarettes outside. They stayed at home in the dark or with blackout curtains tightly covering every window, so that not a crack of light shined through. With a city blacked out at night, enemy bombers wouldn't be able to see it.

Cities also held air raid drills. These were practice sessions to prepare for an enemy attack. When the air-raid siren sounded,

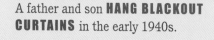

A father and son **HANG BLACKOUT CURTAINS** in the early 1940s.

Following the attack on Pearl Harbor, Americans feared further attacks. People in West Coast cities worried about additional Japanese bombings. Those on the East Coast feared the Germans. people rushed to take cover in designated bomb shelters. School basements often served as shelters, as did subway stations.

In Washington, D.C., Secret Service staff took special steps to protect the president. Workers placed sandbags and machine guns at all White House entrances. They built a bomb shelter underneath the East Wing of the White House. The Secret Service wanted to mount antiaircraft guns on the roofs of government buildings. But the army was short on guns. So the Secret Service made do in some cases with wooden replicas, designed to at least fool the enemy.

The Civil Air Patrol was an important civil defense unit. This organization consisted of about eighty thousand amateur pilots. They flew their own planes along the nation's coastlines, looking for enemy submarines and airplanes. They also flew other missions, such as delivering blood donations and supplies for the military.

To some extent, many civil defense efforts were unnecessary. German and Japanese airplanes never attacked the U.S. mainland. As the war went on, Americans grew less and less worried about attacks. Air raid drills and blackouts became less and less common.

Pilots work on planes at a **CIVIL AIR PATROL BASE** in Bar Harbor, Maine, in 1943.

AMERICA IN THE 1940s

CONSCIENTIOUS OBJECTORS
Art Cramer *(left)*, Phil Stanley *(center)*, and Dave Ratigan battled forest fires in Montana instead of fighting in World War II.

For some draft-age men, World War II presented a dilemma. These were men who had a religious, ethical, or political objection to killing their fellow human beings. Most of them belonged to pacifist churches, such as the Religious Society of Friends, or Quakers, which preach that killing another human is wrong. Men who were pacifists wanted to help the United States win the war—they just didn't want to kill.

In 1940 leaders of three pacifist churches made an arrangement with the U.S. government. The government allowed draft-age pacifists—called conscientious objectors (COs)—to perform alternative service during wartime. Some COs worked at Civilian Public Service (CPS) camps, where they planted trees, fought fires, built roads, and did other outdoor work. Other COs worked at mental institutions or served as "human guinea pigs" for government medical experiments. Many COs served in the armed forces in noncombat jobs. They worked as chaplains (religious counselors) and medics. They wore uniforms like other soldiers but did not carry weapons. The medics, in particular, frequently came under enemy fire. Altogether about thirty-seven thousand men were conscientious objectors during World War II.

The general public did not understand or respect conscientious objectors. Many Americans thought that a man who didn't want to fight was a "yellow belly," or coward. At one store near a CPS camp, a sign warned: "No skunks allowed! So you... conscientious objectors keep the H _ _ _ out of this shop!"

The COs endured the abuse and diligently continued with their work. Their contributions were great. Many CO medics earned medals for their wartime achievements. COs in medical experiments helped doctors learn more about hepatitis, malaria, typhus, and other diseases. COs at mental institutions introduced more humane treatment methods and later helped create the National Mental Health Foundation. Many COs continued work in the peace movement in the decades following World War II.

■ TRIMMING THE FAT

Rationing and wartime shortages forced people to scrimp and save. To save gas, department stores cut back on home deliveries. They urged shoppers to "buy it today and carry it away." Dairies cut their milk deliveries from daily to every other day. Some even delivered milk in horse-drawn wagons. To get to work, people formed carpools and took buses and other mass transportation.

Early in the war, Japan had conquered much of Southeast Asia, cutting off U.S. rubber supplies (which came from the region's rubber trees). To get rubber for tires (for tanks, trucks, and other military vehicles), the U.S. government asked civilians to hold "rubber drives." People searched their basements and garages for scrap rubber: worn-out automobile tires, inner tubes, galoshes, girdles, hot-water bottles, garden hoses, balls, and tire swings. In one wartime publicity stunt, President Roosevelt's Scottish terrier, Fala, proudly donated his rubber bones to a rubber drive.

Metals—zinc, tin, nickel, and steel—were essential to the war effort. So there was little left over for making household products such as bicycles, toasters, typewriters, vacuum cleaners, and lunch boxes. In fact, the WPB banned the manufacture of many such nonessential products.

As they did with rubber, Americans pitched in to collect metal for the military. Schoolchildren held junk drives. They collected tin cans, old pots and pans, buckets, rusted bicycles, and old mattress springs from their neighbors. People also collected bacon grease and other cooking fats. These ingredients were used to make explosives.

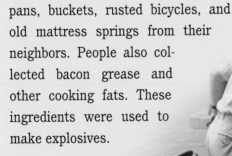

A boy adds to a pile of **SALVAGED RUBBER**. Rubber was one of many items collected for the war effort.

ON THE MOVE AT HOME

During the war years, many civilians relocated. About 27 million moved from small hometowns to big cities, where high-paying jobs were readily available. Washington, D.C., the nation's capital, grew faster than any other city in the country. More than five thousand new government workers poured into the capital each month, many bringing their families with them. The West Coast, with its many shipyards and aircraft plants, also saw a huge increase in population. Between 1940 and 1945, California grew by 2 million people. The populations of Washington and Oregon grew by more than 30 percent.

As the workers came flooding in, cities grew crowded. There weren't nearly enough apartments, rooms for rent, or houses for all the workers and families that needed them. Near

During the war years, many civilians relocated. About 27 million moved from small hometowns to big cities, where high-paying jobs were readily available.

defense plants, some rooming houses rented beds in shifts. One renter would get up early for the morning shift at a defense plant. When he or she left for work, the house owner would quickly air the room, change the sheets, and rent the bed to another worker coming off the graveyard shift. Private home owners rented out extra rooms, often charging exorbitant prices for rooms no bigger than closets. People shared bathrooms with strangers. Enterprising builders constructed flimsy housing units—and rented all of them before the last nail was pounded in.

DOWNTIME

Despite the upheaval, Americans clung to familiar routines and pastimes during the war years. At home—wherever that home might be—they played checkers and chess. Card games, especially bridge, were popular. Americans listened to the radio, both for war news and for entertainment. Regardless of wartime paper shortages, people read books, magazines, and newspapers. Many children "played war," pretending to fire antiaircraft guns as imaginary German Messerschmitts whirred overhead. Many women spent their free hours knitting sweaters for soldiers.

After Japan attacked Pearl Harbor in 1941, an anti-Japanese hysteria gripped the United States. The military kicked out Japanese American soldiers. California revoked the business licenses of five thousand Japanese immigrants. Some Americans accused Japanese Americans of being spies for Japan. The hatred and suspicion were most pronounced on the West Coast, where most Japanese Americans lived.

Two months after the December 7, 1941, attack, President Roosevelt signed executive order 9066. The order gave army generals the authority to evacuate all people of Japanese ancestry from the West Coast. The army moved the evacuees to camps in California, Arizona, Idaho, Wyoming, and Arkansas.

Altogether, the army uprooted 112,353 people from their homes, schools, and jobs. More than 60 percent of the evacuees were U.S. citizens. With just a few weeks' notice, Japanese Americans had to sell their businesses, farms, homes, and possessions. Desperate, one family sold its home and furniture for just $50. A Japanese American farmer sold $80,000 worth of farm equipment for only $6,000. Some families simply abandoned their homes and businesses.

At each relocation camp, about ten thousand Japanese Americans lived in tar paper barracks. They slept on army-style cots, shared toilet facilities, and ate in big mess halls. People carried on as best they could. Children attended camp schools. The

THIS EVACUATED JAPANESE AMERICAN FAMILY wears identification tags around their necks.

government assigned adults to camp jobs or had them work on nearby farms.

The military, needing soldiers, offered Japanese American men a chance to leave the camps and join the military in early 1943. Some men joined because they were eager to get out of the camps. Others were eager to show their patriotism to the United States—despite the discrimination they endured.

Also in 1943, the government let about thirty thousand evacuees leave the camps and take war-related jobs. In late 1944, the U.S. Supreme Court ruled that the relocation program was unconstitutional. One by one, the camps shut down.

To compensate evacuees for their losses, in 1948 Congress granted them payments of up to twenty-five hundred dollars apiece. But this money was only a fraction of the actual losses evacuees had sustained. In 1988 the federal government finally issued a formal apology for the unlawful imprisonment of Japanese Americans. It gave the survivors another twenty thousand dollars each.

69

Religious worship provided a solace for many Americans, especially those who lost loved ones during the war. After the war, religion remained just as important. A 1948 survey revealed that about 69 percent of Americans were Protestant and 22 percent were Catholic. The remaining 9 percent practiced Judaism and other religions. As young families settled into their new suburban homes after the war, people joined churches, synagogues, and other religious organizations in large numbers.

■ WOMEN AT WAR

Women were not drafted during World War II, nor were they allowed to join the regular U.S. military. Instead, tens of thousands joined special women's military units—the Women's Army Corps (WAC), the navy's Women Accepted for Volunteer Emergency Service (WAVES), the Women Marines, and the Coast Guard's SPARS. Thousands more became army or navy nurses.

ARMY NURSES POSE ON A JEEP IN FRANCE IN 1944. Many American women served overseas during World War II.

A FEMALE CAB DRIVER GETS READY TO TAKE A FARE. During World War II, American women held many jobs that were not available to them before the war.

None of these women held combat jobs. Mostly, the military used them behind the scenes, doing office work for instance. Still, some servicewomen—especially nurses—worked close to the front lines of battle. More than two hundred army nurses were killed on the job.

One little-known military unit consisted of 1,830 female pilots, who trained at Avenger Field near Sweetwater, Texas, in 1943. They were members of the Women Airforce Service Pilots (WASP) program. They trained not as fighter pilots but as service pilots. In this role, they tested new military airplanes, ferried aircraft from factories to bases, shuttled troops and cargo, and towed targets for artillery practice. Thirty-eight of these women lost their lives when their planes went down. Their role in the war was kept quiet because many male pilots felt that women shouldn't be flying airplanes at all.

Far outnumbering the females in uniform, more than 2.3 million women worked in war industries. Before the war, men had been the nation's primary workers outside the home. Men were the bus drivers, farmers, factory workers, mechanics, delivery drivers, and airplane pilots. When the men left for war, many women took over these jobs.

Between 1940 and 1945, the number of women working outside the home jumped from almost 12 million to more than 18.5 million. Women made up 12 percent of the workforce in shipyards and 10 percent in aircraft assembly plants. One young woman from Connecticut remembered her job in an aircraft plant:

> They put me into a training program for about two months. . . . Oh, I was so pleased with myself; it was for the war effort. I got this certified machinist certificate, and I was so proud. . . . The [aircraft] factory covered miles. You'd check in, and then you'd walk and walk and walk and walk until you got to your own little niche. It was very exciting. I ran a Norton OD grinder. . . . We would grind parts that would go into the Pratt and Whitney engines. . . . [The factory] was like a small town all under this one roof. . . . I got into the night shift. . . . It was always exciting to drive up at eleven-thirty at night. From a distance you could see the plant, all the anti-aircraft lights on the roof, and you just felt like you were involved.

Soldiers returning from war had no trouble finding jobs in shipyards and other defense businesses. When companies hired returning men, however, they usually fired the women (and African Americans) who had served as wartime staff. Women were upset by this discrimination. But during that era, there were no equal employment laws to protect their rights in the workplace. "It was a great blow," recalled one woman who lost her high-paying shipbuilding job when the war ended. "I know the pride I had felt during the war. I just felt ten feet [3 m] tall. Here I was doing an important job, and doing it well, and then all at once here comes V-J [Victory in Japan] Day . . . and I'm back making homemade bread."

■ HOME SWEET HOME

Women returned to homemaker roles by the thousands after World War II. Returning servicemen were eager to reunite with and marry their sweethearts. Marriage rates soared—and so did birthrates. The baby boom—a postwar population explosion—officially began on January 1, 1946. Social scientists refer to Kathleen Casey as the nation's first baby boomer. She was born in Philadelphia, Pennsylvania, one second past midnight on that day.

> **"I know the pride I had felt during the war. I just felt ten feet [3 m] tall. Here I was doing an important job, and doing it well, and then all at once here comes V-J [Victory in Japan] Day . . . and I'm back making homemade bread."**

—female shipbuilder who lost her job following World War II

Before World War II, married couples had kept their families small. It wasn't possible to feed and care for a lot of children in the Depression years. But with post–World War II prosperity, families of five, six, and even more children became commonplace. In his best-selling *Common Sense Book of Baby and Child Care*, Dr. Benjamin Spock encouraged new parents to "be natural and comfortable, and enjoy your baby."

A RETURNING SOLDIER greets his wife, child, and neighbors.

73

Newlywed soldiers and their families needed places to live. But the housing shortage that occurred during wartime did not let up afterward. Young families crowded into basements, attics, and rented rooms. Universities, faced with a flood of veterans on the GI Bill, housed students in trailers and other prefab houses [made by easy assembly].

In Hempstead, Long Island, New York, builder William Levitt saw a moneymaking opportunity. Taking advantage of the housing shortage, Levitt constructed more than seventeen thousand simple, inexpensive, and nearly identical Cape Cod- and ranch-style houses on the site of a former potato field, 25 miles (40 km) east of New York City. Using prefabricated parts and assembly-line techniques, Levitt was able to construct twenty to thirty homes a day.

SUBURBAN DEVELOPMENTS sprang up on the outskirts of big U.S. cities after the war.

He named his new neighborhood Levittown—after himself. Costing as little as $6,990 apiece, the homes immediately filled up with young families. (They were all white families, since Levitt refused to sell to African Americans.) The Levittown model spread across the United States, with similar suburban developments mushrooming on the edges of many big cities.

Once settled in, families set out to enjoy U.S. prosperity. They bought washing machines, new cars (with tail fins—a design flair introduced in 1949), and every other product they had done without during wartime. They bought new television sets and new air conditioners. At last, hard times had ended in the United States. Americans were happy to enjoy the long-awaited good life. For returning soldiers, that meant marriage, children, and a home of one's own.

U.S. soldiers read copies of *NEWSWEEK AND LIFE* magazines
on the battlefields of Burma during World War II.

CHAPTER SIX

A GOOD **BOOK:**
LITERATURE OF THE 1940s

In the pre-TV 1940s, people devoted many hours a week to reading. Young and old read everything from romance novels and poetry to biographies, newspapers, and popular magazines.

When war came, paper grew scarce, because the ingredients used in papermaking—things such as chlorine and wood pulp—went to make military necessities. During scrap drives, children routinely collected scrap paper along with pots, pans, and cooking fats.

Even so, Americans didn't give up books during the war. To economize with the printed page, publishers used smaller margins, thinner paper, and smaller type. Paperbacks, introduced to the United States by the Pocket Book Company in 1939, were a cheap alternative to expensive hardbound books.

Early in the 1940s, novelists who had made their reputations in earlier decades continued to write highly acclaimed works. William Faulkner, most famous for his novels about the southern United States, continued that tradition with *Go Down, Moses* (1942). Ernest Hemingway, noted for his tough male characters and punchy prose, examined the Spanish Civil War of the late 1930s in *For Whom the Bell Tolls* (1940). John Steinbeck, Pearl Buck, William Saroyan, and Henry Miller were other award-winning writers who remained prolific in the 1940s.

New novelists debuted as the decade began. Carson McCullers impressed the critics with *The Heart Is a Lonely Hunter* in 1940. She followed that up with *Reflections in a Golden Eye* (1941) and *The Member of the Wedding* (1946). McCullers was a native of Columbus, Georgia, and her works explored small-town southern life. Eudora Welty, also a southerner, arrived on the literary scene in 1942 with a well-received short novel, *The Robber Bridegroom.* A longer work, *Delta Wedding* (1946), was equally acclaimed.

Richard Wright broke new ground by exploring the African American experience at a time when black voices were rarely heard in U.S. literature. In *Native Son* (1940), Wright tells the story of Bigger Thomas, a young Chicago man whose grim surroundings lead him to a desperate act of murder. Wright continued to reveal the African American experience in the autobiographical *Black Boy* (1945) and later works.

■ WRITERS AT WAR

When war came to the United States, Americans hungered for war news. Radio broadcasts, movie newsreels, and local newspapers delivered the latest reports from the battlefields of Europe and the Pacific. To give Americans

AUTHOR RICHARD WRIGHT sits at his typewriter in 1945. Wright captured the African American experience in novels such as *Native Son* and *Black Boy*.

LEFT: REPORTER MARGUERITE HIGGINS went to Europe to cover World War II in 1944.
RIGHT: WAR CORRESPONDENT ERNIE PYLE *(left)* talks with photographer J. R. Eyerman
shortly before the pair left for Okinawa in 1945.

the most accurate information possible, broadcasters and news organizations dispatched reporters to the front lines. Some writers, including Ernest Hemingway and essayist A. J. Liebling, arrived on the beaches of France with the D-day invasion force. Marguerite Higgins, writing for the *New York Tribune*, covered the fall of Nazi Germany, the liberation of concentration camps, and the Nuremberg Trials.

The most famous war correspondent was Indianan Ernie Pyle. A columnist for the Scripps Howard newspaper chain, Pyle traveled with Allied troops in North Africa, Europe, and the Pacific. His battlefront dispatches appeared in hundreds of daily and weekly newspapers back in the United States. Pyle offered readers a "foxhole view" of the war—the view of the ordinary soldier. He described one group of GIs this way:

> They seemed terribly pathetic to me. They weren't warriors. They were American boys who by mere change of fate had wound up with guns in their hands sneaking up a death-laden street in a strange and shattered city in a faraway country in a driving rain. They were afraid, but it was beyond their power to quit. They had no choice. . . . And even though they aren't warriors born to the kill, they win their battles. That's the point.

Like many of the men he wrote about, Pyle died from enemy fire. A Japanese machine gun bullet killed him on the Pacific island of Ie Shima during the Okinawa campaign of 1945. Pyle's wartime writings were compiled into four books: *Ernie Pyle in England* (1941), *Here Is Your War* (1943), *Brave Men* (1944), and *Last Chapter* (1946).

Like the public back in the States, soldiers devoured reading materials, including letters and paperback books sent from home. The U.S. Army produced two publications just for soldiers: *Stars and Stripes*, a daily newspaper, and *Yank*, a weekly magazine. Both publications included war coverage, feature stories, photos, cartoons, and other material of interest to soldiers. Many leading journalists launched their careers with one publication or the other.

Americans at home and at war read **COMIC BOOKS**, such as the Wonder Woman *(right, launched in 1943),* Batman, and Captain America series, in huge numbers.

Wartime is often a time of censorship. Officers read soldiers' letters to make sure they don't contain military secrets. Governments slant the news in their favor. All this happened in the United States during World War II. But World War II was also a time to celebrate the U.S. ideal of freedom of speech.

In 1933 in Germany, the Nazis had banned and burned books, destroying about twenty thousand works that they considered to be "un-German." Americans were appalled. After Pearl Harbor, freedom of the press and freedom of speech became rallying points for Americans at war.

Three groups took the lead in this effort. The Writers' War Board was a private group of writers, organized to use their literary talents in the war effort. Members wrote patriotic slogans, poems, radio plays, and government publications. In 1942 and 1943, the board sponsored anniversary observances of the Nazi book burnings to remind Americans of the evils of Nazi ideology. The board also compiled a list of the burned and banned books and encouraged people to read them. A second group, the Council on Books in Wartime, was formed by leading library, publishing, and educational organizations. Adopting the slogan "Books Are Weapons in the War of Ideas," the council organized book drives and book fairs. It published paper-

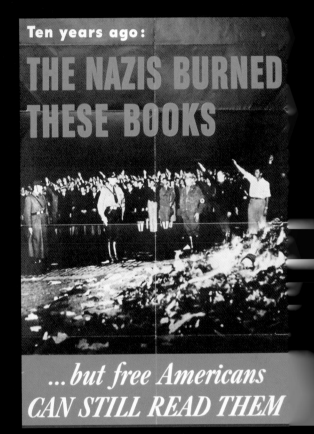

Ten years ago:

THE NAZIS BURNED THESE BOOKS

...but free Americans CAN STILL READ THEM

THE OFFICE OF WAR INFORMATION created this poster and others like it to encourage Americans to embrace freedom of speech and fight against those who didn't.

back books, including those banned and burned by the Nazis, and distributed them free to U.S. soldiers. Finally, the Office of War Information, a federal agency, used the press, radio, movies, and other media to promote the Allied cause. Together, these three groups promoted books and reading as American virtues.

The military experience provided plenty of material for novelists both during and after the war. Chicagoan Saul Bellow was a prolific writer of the mid- to late twentieth century. His first novel, *Dangling Man* (1944), illuminates the thoughts and feelings of a young man as he waits for his army induction. By far the most famous World War II novel was *The Naked and the Dead* (1948) by Norman Mailer. Set on a steamy Pacific island, Mailer's work reveals the war experience in all its brutality and tragedy. James Jones, Herman Wouk, and Irwin Shaw were other novelists who used World War II as a canvas for works of literature.

John Hersey was a war correspondent who wrote both fiction and nonfiction books about World War II. His nonfiction *Hiroshima* (1946) describes the destruction of that city by the U.S. atomic bomb. Also nonfiction, *Men on Bataan* (1942) provides Hersey's firsthand observations of the war. Hersey won a Pulitzer Prize for *A Bell for Adano*, a 1945 novel about U.S. GIs who occupy an Italian village.

Ted Lawson's *Thirty Seconds over Tokyo* was an immediate best seller when it hit bookstands in 1943. The book tells the exciting tale of the Doolittle Raid—a surprise Allied attack on Tokyo in April 1942. Lawson was one of the air force flyers who made the raid. Many of his fellow raiders didn't survive to tell the story.

NORMAN MAILER, shown here in 1948, wrote the famous war novel *The Naked and the Dead*.

■ UP AND COMING

In the late 1940s, with the war over and the United States entering a new era of peace and prosperity, new voices emerged on the literary scene. One belonged to Truman Capote. This bright young southerner took the literary world by storm in 1948 with the publication of *Other Voices, Other Rooms,* a poignant coming-of-age tale. J. D. Salinger was another impressive young voice. His 1940s short stories, mostly published in the *New Yorker* magazine, served as a warm-up for his brilliant novels of the 1950s. Salinger's main characters were frequently teenagers, and his keen take on youthful sensibilities earned him many young adult fans. Paul Bowles, James Michener, Shirley Jackson, and Ray Bradbury were other new names who emerged in the late 1940s and found success in the following decades.

AUTHOR TRUMAN CAPOTE works on a novel at an artist's community in New York State in 1946.

Raymond Chandler was one of the most popular authors of the 1940s. His "hard-boiled" detective fiction will forever be associated with the decade. He was born in Chicago, Illinois, but raised in Great Britain. Returning to the United States as a young man, he settled in Los Angeles, taking jobs at a variety of businesses.

In the 1930s, he found his true gift—writing detective stories. His works appeared in the magazines *Black Mask*, *Detective Fiction Weekly*,

RAYMOND CHANDLER created tough-talking detectives in both books and movies.

and *Dime Detective*. His first novel, *The Big Sleep*, came out in 1939. That was followed quickly by *Farewell My Lovely* (1940), *The High Window* (1942), *The Lady in the Lake* (1943), *The Little Sister* (1949), *The Long Goodbye* (1953), and *Playback* (1958).

Many of Chandler's books followed the adventures of the hard-drinking, tough-talking private eye Philip Marlowe. He regularly delivered winning lines such as "Dead men are heavier than broken hearts" (*The Big Sleep*); "It was a blonde. A blonde to make a bishop kick a hole in a stained glass window" (*Farewell My Lovely*); and "I

needed a drink, I needed a lot of life insurance, I needed a vacation, I needed a home in the country. What I had was a coat, a hat and gun" (*Farewell My Lovely*).

Several of Chandler's books were made into Hollywood movies. He also wrote screenplays for what became classic movies, including *Double Indemnity* (1944), *Blue Dahlia* (1946), and *Strangers on a Train* (1951). Chandler died in 1959, but his brilliance lives on in his tales of bad guys, fall guys, femme fatales, double-crossers, and other colorful characters.

As the U.S. baby population boomed in the late 1940s, a number of writers fed young imaginations with stories and picture books. The famous Dr. Seuss published *McElligot's Pool* and the lesser-known *Thidwick the Big-Hearted Moose* in the late 1940s. E. B. White's *Stuart Little,* the tale of a mouse with a human family, came out in 1945. *Goodnight Moon,* the classic bedtime story by Margaret Wise Brown, arrived in 1947.

Magazines had long been popular in U.S. households. *Life, Look,* and the *Saturday Evening Post* were family favorites in the 1940s. *Ladies' Home Journal* and *Good Housekeeping* spoke to the woman of the house. In 1944 a new magazine debuted. It was *Seventeen,* written just for teenage girls. With articles on fashion, grooming, and dating, *Seventeen* was a must-have for young females. *Ebony* magazine hit newsstands one year later, in 1945. The brainchild of publisher John Harold Johnson, *Ebony* targeted an African American audience.

MARGARET WISE BROWN'S books, such as *Goodnight Moon* and *The Runaway Bunny*, have become classics.

Joe Rosenthal took this photograph of U.S. troops RAISING THE FLAG AT THE TOP OF MOUNT SURIBACHI ON IWO JIMA IN 1945. The image immediately became a visual symbol of World War II.

CHAPTER SEVEN

AMERICAN SCENE:
ART, ARCHITECTURE, AND FASHION

Every decade leaves behind its dramatic images. But the images of the 1940s were particularly searing. In many cases, they were images of war, death, and destruction. Even artwork that was not directly related to combat still reflected the feelings and fears of a nation at war.

■ CAUGHT ON FILM

By the 1940s, photography was a well-established journalistic tool. Photographers of the 1940s captured grim scenes of warfare with their cameras. They delivered these pictures through daily newspapers and magazines such as *Look* and *Life*.

Americans at home didn't have to wonder what the Allied landing on the beaches of Normandy looked like. When the infantry landed on Omaha Beach on June 6, 1944, *Life* photographer Robert Capa was there with his camera. When the marines raised the U.S. flag atop Mount Suribachi on Iwo Jima on February 23, 1945, Associated Press photographer Joe Rosenthal captured the dramatic scene.

Capa, Rosenthal, and other war photographers took pictures of servicemen in the field, the bombed-out cities of Europe and Japan, civilians fleeing their homes, Allied leaders, and planes and warships being readied for battle. Color photography was new and still uncommon in the 1940s, so most of the war photographers shot in black and white. Their photographs offer stark scenes of life, death, and desperation.

87

One of the most famous photographs from World War II was taken atop 550-foot (168 m) Mount Suribachi, a volcanic mountain on the Pacific island of Iwo Jima. The photographer was Joe Rosenthal.

During World War II, Rosenthal worked for the Associated Press (AP), a news-gathering association. He was assigned to cover the war in the Pacific. On February 23, 1945, he was working alongside Allied troops on Iwo Jima, four days after their landing there. That morning someone told him that the marines were raising a U.S. flag on Mount Suribachi, an important piece of high ground that the U.S. troops had recently captured.

Rosenthal hurried up the mountain with some other photographers. On his way up, he learned that the flag had already been raised, but he continued on. As it turned out, commanders decided to take down the first flag and put up a larger one. Rosenthal shot a photo just as a group of five marines

and a navy corpsman were straining to put the big flag into place.

Two days later, the photograph was on the cover of Sunday newspapers across the United States. Americans were greatly moved by the patriotic scene. The image was even more heart-wrenching because by the time the thirty-six-day battle for Iwo Jima was over, almost seven thousand U.S. servicemen— including three of the flag raisers—had died.

U.S. leaders quickly recognized the importance of Rosenthal's image as a propaganda tool. The government plastered it on millions of posters as part of a war bond drive. The post office printed the image on postage stamps. The marines later used it as a model for the Marine Corps War Memorial in Arlington, Virginia.

Eddie Adams, an AP photographer of later wars, said that Rosenthal's photo was perfect: "The position, the body language. . . . You couldn't set anything up like this—it's just so perfect." Rosenthal won a Pulitzer Prize for the photograph in 1945.

■ "THIS IS THE ENEMY"

During the war years, most Americans were extremely patriotic. People on the home front pitched in any way they could—by buying war bonds, collecting scrap metal, knitting sweaters for soldiers, and volunteering for civil defense work. To make sure this patriotic spirit didn't wane, the U.S. government egged Americans on with propaganda posters. Propaganda is communication—a movie, a political advertisement, a radio broadcast, or another type of message—designed to influence people's thinking and actions.

The Office of War Information, the War Production Board, and other government agencies printed thousands of propaganda posters during World War II. The posters hung in workplaces, subways, schools, government offices, and other public places. Their purpose was always the same—to rally Americans behind the war effort and to remind them of their duties as U.S. citizens.

One poster showed a U.S. soldier encouraging a farmer: "These overalls are your uniform, bud." In other words, growing food was just as important to the country as fighting on the battlefield. Another poster showed a female factory worker with a kerchief on her head, her shirtsleeves rolled up, and her hand tightened into a fist. She was the mythical Rosie the Riveter, a nickname for female defense workers. "We can do it," Rosie says through a cartoon speech bubble. With these words, she tells women working in defense plants and shipyards that they are tough enough and skilled enough to carry out the big job of building weapons.

Some posters warned civilians to keep quiet about military information, because one never knew if spies were listening. To hammer home this message, one poster showed a sailor chest-deep in the ocean at night. Clearly, the enemy has destroyed

We Can Do It!

WAR PRODUCTION CO-ORDINATING COMMITTEE

The U.S. government's **ROSIE THE RIVETER** poster is a classic example of wartime propaganda.

his ship in the inky black waters. He raises his finger accusingly and says, "Someone talked." In other words, someone leaked a military secret—leading to the ship's sinking and most likely the death of the poor sailor and his brothers-in-arms. Other propaganda posters urged men to enlist in the armed forces, housewives to grow and can their own vegetables, and war workers to set aside their racial differences.

U.S. propaganda posters were not subtle. They frequently showed Germans and Japanese as bloodthirsty and sinister. In one image, a grotesque Japanese soldier, dagger in hand, sneaks up behind a terrified young American woman. "This is the enemy," warns the poster. Another picture shows the arm of a Nazi soldier. The dreaded Nazi symbol, the swastika, adorns his sleeve. His hand is bloody. It grips a knife that has pierced straight through the sacred Bible. Again, the caption reads, "This is the enemy." In yet another scene, a two-headed monster—one head German and the other Japanese—stands with a knife in one hand. With the other hand, the monster has ripped the Statue of Liberty off its pedestal. Meanwhile, in the foreground, the

PROPAGANDA POSTERS often used fear and other strong emotions to stir U.S. patriotism.

hand of an American grips a wrench, readied like a club to hit the monster. The wrench is labeled "production." The text explains: "Stop this monster that stops at nothing. Produce [weapons and military equipment] to the limit! This is your war."

Norman Rockwell was a beloved U.S. illustrator of the mid-twentieth century. He created charming and sometimes humorous scenes of small-town life in the United States. His pictures frequently graced the cover of the popular magazine *Saturday Evening Post*. During World War II, Rockwell turned his artistic talents to patriotic scenes. His version of *Rosie the Riveter* shows an overall-clad Rosie with her rivet gun on her lap. She munches on a sandwich at the factory with an enormous U.S. flag flowing behind her. Rockwell's Four Freedoms poster series showed ordinary Americans relishing and expressing their precious freedom of speech, freedom of worship, freedom from fear, and freedom from want. The *Freedom from Fear* poster shows a loving mom and dad tucking their angelic-faced son and daughter into bed. Dad holds a newspaper with headlines of frightening war developments—yet the scene is one of security and love. The text on the Four Freedoms posters encouraged Americans to buy war bonds and reminded them that these freedoms were "ours . . . to fight for."

OURS...to fight for

FREEDOM FROM WANT

Even comic books and comic strips peddled patriotism during wartime. *Joe Palooka* was a popular newspaper comic strip created by Hammond Fisher. Its title character, Joe, was the heavyweight boxing champ. But when war came, Joe gave up the chance to earn big money boxing in Cuba. Instead, he joined the U.S. Army. Comic strip detective Dick Tracy joined naval intelligence.

The comic character Little Orphan Annie was too young

NORMAN ROCKWELL created the Four Freedoms poster series, including *Freedom from Want (left)* in 1943.

to join one of the women's branches of the U.S. military, but she was old enough to organize the Junior Commando movement. In this organization, Annie and her pals collected newspapers, scrap metal, cooking fats, and other sought-after items. She also inspired real U.S. children to set up their own Junior Commando units at schools and community centers.

Then there was Wonder Woman. This comic-book character didn't need an organized unit to fight the Nazis. With her star-spangled costume and superhuman strength, she single-handedly took on sinister Nazi agents.

Two of the most famous comic strips of the 1940s appeared in military publications. *Stars and Stripes* ran the *Up Front* cartoons by Bill Mauldin. This strip featured the wartime frustrations of fictional GIs Willie and Joe. *Yank* magazine ran *Sad Sack*. Created by George Baker, this comic strip similarly recounted the day-to-day struggles of a lowly GI. Both cartoons were extremely popular with real GIs, who knew all too well the hassles of real army life.

BILL MAULDIN holds a drawing board with some of his *Up Front* characters. He won the Pulitzer Prize for his cartoons in 1945.

JACKSON POLLOCK works on a painting in 1948. Finished paintings are propped up behind him.

■ HIGH ART

The abstract expressionists—a New York–based group of mostly U.S. artists—caused a sensation with a radically new kind of painting in the mid-1940s. They didn't paint realistic landscapes, objects, or scenes of everyday life. Instead, they explored the act of painting and the physical qualities of paint—the way it sat, splattered, and pooled on the canvas. One of the best-known abstract expressionists was Wyoming-born Jackson Pollock. Emphasizing process and spontaneity, he placed his canvases on the floor and dripped paint on them from above.

Affected in part by the darkness of World War II, the abstract expressionists used their paintings to expose the hidden, inner struggles of the human mind. With their often large, colorful canvases, they offered a new form of self-expression and a new way of looking at the world. Other abstract expressionists of the 1940s included Robert Motherwell and Mark Rothko.

> **❝ To us, art is an adventure into an unknown world of the imagination which is fancy-free and violently opposed to common sense. ❞**
>
> —*Adolph Gottlieb and Barnett Newman,*
> *abstract expressionists, 1943*

It's not often that people find fame at the age of eighty, but Grandma Moses did just that. Her original name was Anna Robertson. Born in 1860, she grew up on a farm in rural New York State and had only a few months of schooling as a child. She married Thomas Moses in 1887 and worked alongside him as a farmer in Virginia and then back in New York State. After Thomas died in 1927, Anna continued to farm with the help of her son.

GRANDMA MOSES mixes colors at her farm in Hoosick Falls, New York, in 1946.

When she retired from farming in 1936, her life took an interesting turn. Moses took up painting, a hobby she had enjoyed during childhood. On fiberboard, she painted scenes of rural life—pictures of maple sugaring, apple picking, holidays, farm animals, and family fun. In 1939 an art dealer named Louis Caldor saw some of Moses's paintings in a drugstore window in Hoosick Falls, New York. He was impressed. Here was a self-taught folk artist, capturing vivid scenes of U.S. country life. The paintings were colorful and charming. Caldor bought fifteen of them.

Later that year, he arranged to show three of the paintings at an exhibition at the Museum of Modern Art in New York City. Art critics couldn't get enough. In 1940 Moses held a one-woman show of thirty-five paintings at a New York gallery. At the age of eighty, "Grandma Moses" had become an art world star. Moses lived to be 101. By then she had made more than sixteen hundred paintings.

Other artists also pushed the visual world into new directions in the 1940s. A shy and reclusive New Yorker, Joseph Cornell impressed the critics with his sculptures, collages, and films. Influenced by surrealist artists, Cornell assembled everyday items, such as photographs and objects from secondhand stores, to create miniature fantasy worlds.

In architecture the leading U.S. innovator was Philip Johnson. In the 1930s, Johnson had headed the architecture department at the Museum of Modern Art in New York. There, he embraced the minimalist style of architecture. Minimalism in architecture involves revealing a building's basic structure as part of its visual appeal. In the 1940s, Johnson became an architect himself. His first famous project was his own home in New Canaan, Connecticut, built in 1949. Called the Glass House, it was a glass building with an exposed steel frame. The Glass House launched Johnson's career and established him as one of the greatest architects of the twentieth century.

■ MONUMENTAL

In the 1940s, several big monuments emerged on the U.S. landscape. One, the Mount Rushmore National Memorial, had been in the works for almost two decades. Mount Rushmore is a granite cliff near Keystone, South Dakota. On it are carved the profiles of four U.S. presidents: George Washington, Thomas Jefferson, Abraham Lincoln, and Theodore Roosevelt. Sculptor Gutzon Borglum was in charge of designing and carving the monument. He and his crew started carving in 1927. When Borglum

died in 1941, his son Lincoln took over the project. By then the monument was almost completed. Gutzon Borglum had originally planned to carve the figures down to their waists. But the money for the project ran out, and Lincoln Borglum couldn't convince the federal government to give him anymore. So on October 31, 1941, carving officially ended. At that time, the United States was most worried about World War II, so Mount Rushmore's completion got little attention.

The government undertook another big construction project in the early 1940s. It was a giant office building—the Pentagon—headquarters of the U.S. War Department (later renamed the Department of Defense). Construction began in September 1941, right before the United States entered World War II. With banks of lights burning throughout the night, thirteen thousand workers toiled around the clock to build it. Located in Arlington, Virginia, across the Potomac River from Washington, D.C., the building was completed in January 1943. The massive five-sided structure cost $83 million to build.

Another monument completed in the 1940s was the Jefferson Memorial. This impressive, white marble

This photograph shows **THE JEFFERSON MEMORIAL** under construction in 1941.

building in Washington, D.C., honors Thomas Jefferson, the third president of the United States. Work on the memorial began in 1938 and ended in 1943. On April 13, 1943, the two hundredth anniversary of Jefferson's birth, the federal government held a dedication ceremony. President Roosevelt addressed the crowd. "Today, in the midst of a great war for freedom," Roosevelt said, "we dedicate a shrine to freedom." The memorial was especially inspirational in a time of war.

THE FORTIES LOOK

At the 1939 World's Fair in New York City, a model named Miss Chemistry introduced nylon stockings. Cheaper and easier to care for than traditional silk stockings, nylons were a hit with female shoppers. But when the United States entered World War II,

DuPont stopped making the stockings. Instead, DuPont used nylon (and silk) to make parachutes for the military. What did women do then? As was common during World War II, most women made do without. But some went a step further: using makeup pencil, they drew lines up the back of their legs to look like stocking seams.

Women on the home front were used to such tricks. The government needed nylon, silk, cotton, wool, and leather for soldiers' clothing and equipment. New clothes were hard to come by. So people at home mended and patched old clothes. They wore hand-me-downs and stitched together old pieces of fabric to make new outfits. Since the military needed rubber to make tires, many women stopped wearing rubber girdles.

The government rationed leather shoes: two pairs per person per year. To save fabric, it even passed restrictions on the manufacture of new clothing. According to wartime rules, a woman's skirt could be no wider than 78 inches (198 centimeters) around. Sleeves could measure no more than 14 inches (36 cm) around. Belts had to be less than 2 inches (5 cm) wide. Ruffles, pleats, and extra pockets were banned. Some men wore "victory suits," made without cuffs. For women, trim, knee-length skirts replaced long gowns. Even clothing dyes were scarce. That meant that bright colors were out and black, brown, and white were in.

Some interesting new styles emerged during wartime. For women the military look was trendy. This look included short jackets, narrow skirts, wide shoulders, pantsuits, low-heeled shoes, berets, and peaked caps.

At their factory jobs, women wore work boots, coveralls, overalls, and trousers—clothing that at the time was viewed as unfeminine. Some women wanted to imitate Hollywood bombshell Veronica Lake. Her long blond hair was parted to one side and hung down across her cheek. The look was sexy, but factory bosses worried that long hair would get caught in the machinery. So they banned the Lake look. Female defense workers had to wear their hair short or tucked up into buns, hats, or scarves.

When the war at last ended, clothing restrictions ended too. Nylon sales skyrocketed. Postwar styles for women featured rounded shoulders, long spreading skirts, V-necks, narrow waistlines, flouncy hats, high heels, and bright colors. The bikini bathing suit arrived in 1946, although it revealed too much skin for most U.S. women.

In the 1940s—both before and after the war—people dressed formally. When they left the house to visit friends, see a movie or play, or even watch a baseball game, they usually wore dressy clothing. That meant suits, ties, and hats for men and hats, dresses, gloves, and stockings for women. Casual trousers, sweaters, and jackets were strictly for knocking around the house.

The short jackets, wide shoulders, and narrow skirts of the early 1940s **WERE INSPIRED BY MILITARY UNIFORMS**.

THE PHILADELPHIA STORY is a romantic comedy starring Katharine Hepburn *(right)*, Jimmy Stewart *(third from right)*, and Cary Grant *(not pictured)*.

CHAPTER EIGHT

THE SHOW GOES ON:
THE DRAMATIC ARTS

Moviegoers in 1940 had lots to choose from. Those who wanted laughs that year could watch the side-splitting antics of W. C. Fields in *The Bank Dick*. Kids of 1940 likely preferred *Fantasia* and *Pinocchio*, full-length animated classics from Walt Disney Studios, and the brand-new Bugs Bunny cartoon shorts from Warner Brothers. *Knute Rockne: All American* was a sentimental football biography starring Hollywood hunk (and future U.S. president) Ronald Reagan. *The Mark of Zorro* was a swashbuckling adventure story with the handsome Tyrone Power. For clever dialogue and romance, *The Philadelphia Story* with Katharine Hepburn, Cary Grant, and Jimmy Stewart fit the bill. *His Girl Friday,* pairing Cary Grant with Rosalind Russell, did the same. *Rebecca*, from acclaimed British director Alfred Hitchcock, dished up romance and suspense. For those who wanted to escape to the mythical Old West, *The Westerner* with Gary Cooper was a good choice.

The movies were a good place to forget life's day-to-day struggles and worries. That's why many Americans liked romances, comedies, and fantasies. But not all movies offered escapism in 1940. John Ford's *The Grapes of Wrath*, starring Henry Fonda, reminded Americans of very real-life troubles. Based on the novel of the same name by John

Steinbeck, *The Grapes of Wrath* chronicled the plight of a Depression-era family who leave drought-stricken Oklahoma for what they hope will be a better life in California. The Depression was not yet over in 1940, and for many families, the film struck a chord.

The Depression wasn't the only worry as the decade began. Europe was at war. Free nations were falling one by one to vicious dictators. Earlier in the century, Charlie Chaplin had delighted Americans with his brilliant silent comic films. In 1940 Chaplin returned to the movies in a speaking role. The film was *The Great Dictator.* In this movie, playing both a dictator and a Jewish barber, Chaplin made fun of Adolf Hitler. Audiences chuckled, but the real-life Adolf Hitler was no laughing matter. Americans knew all too well in 1940 that war was on the horizon.

■ HOLLYWOOD GOES TO WAR

War did indeed come, and the U.S. movie industry rallied behind the war effort. In 1942 alone, about eighty Hollywood films dealt with the war in some way. One of the most famous was *Casablanca.* Set in war-torn Morocco in North

HUMPHREY BOGART AND INGRID BERGMAN
played Rick Blaine and Ilsa Lund in *Casablanca.*

No actor played the film noir (brooding crime film) tough guy better than Humphrey Bogart. Bogart had rugged good looks, a gruff voice, and an understated confidence. When it came time to cast the part of a hard-boiled detective or a humble hero, Bogart was the first choice of 1940s film directors.

Born in 1899, Bogart grew up in New York City. His parents wanted him to be a doctor, but Bogart preferred the stage. He acted in small film roles in New York before moving to Hollywood, California, in 1930. Throughout the 1930s, he mostly played gangsters. In the 1940s, Bogart broke out in new directions. He played the sleazy detective Sam Spade in *The Maltese Falcon* in 1942. In *Casablanca*, also in 1942, he played the romantic lead opposite Ingrid Bergman. By then Bogart's appeal as a leading man was sealed. He played opposite Lauren Bacall in *To Have and Have Not* (1944), a classic wartime romance based on a novel by Ernest Hemingway. Bogart and Bacall later married (and made three more films together). Bogart worked nonstop in the 1950s. He won an Oscar for Best Actor for his role as a riverboat captain in *The African Queen* (1951), also starring Katharine Hepburn. He died of cancer in 1957.

Africa, it starred Humphrey Bogart as the cynical nightclub owner Rick Blaine and Ingrid Bergman as an old flame who comes back into Rick's life unexpectedly. *Bataan* (1943), *Guadalcanal Diary* (1943), and *Lifeboat* (1944) were only a few of the numerous World War II movies produced while battles were raging. As the war wound down, the movies kept coming. *The Story of G.I. Joe* (1945) chronicled the frontline experiences of war correspondent Ernie Pyle. *The Best Years of Our Lives* (1946) told the wrenching story of veterans trying to readjust to civilian life after the war.

Young, healthy, and patriotic, many film stars joined the armed forces. They included Henry Fonda, Jimmy Stewart, and Clark Gable, to name just a few. Well-known directors made documentaries about the war. Some stars performed at war bond drives. Others joined forces with the United Services Organization, or USO. The USO sponsored entertainment and recreational activities for soldiers both overseas and at stateside bases. Bob Hope, Jack Benny, Bing Crosby, Lana Turner, Rita Hayworth, and dozens of other big-name

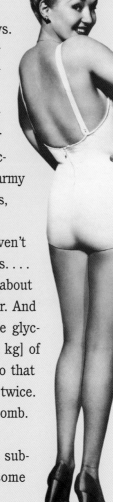

BETTY GRABLE strikes a classic pinup girl pose in 1943.

entertainers sang, danced, and hammed it up at USO shows. Betty Grable and Jane Russell were movie stars, but they earned even more fame as pinup girls—GIs pinned their sexy pictures on the walls of their barracks.

The U.S. government encouraged movie studios to make war movies. After all, they were good propaganda. The Office of War Information produced its own short propaganda films. One fictional short, *A Letter from Bataan,* showed a wounded GI in an army hospital in the Philippines. His letter home to the family pleads,

> For one thing, tell the folks not to hoard food. We haven't had anything but a little horse meat and rice for days.... Tell that friend of yours, Mrs. Jackson, to stop bragging about all the coffee and sugar she's got stored up in her cellar. And kitchen fats, Mom. Don't waste any. Kitchen fats make glycerine and glycerine makes explosives. Two pounds [0.9 kg] of fat can fire five anti-tank shells. And pass this along to that brother-in-law of mine, Ray, who won't use a razor blade twice. It takes 12,000 razor blades for one 2,000-lb. [907 kg] bomb.

As this example shows, the propaganda films were not subtle—and they were effective. Upon viewing OWI films, some audience members wept.

■ "THERE'S NO BUSINESS LIKE SHOW BUSINESS"

In addition to war films, Hollywood continued to make musicals, comedies, romances, and westerns. Orson Welles made and starred in his award-winning *Citizen Kane*—based on the life of publisher William Randolph Hearst—in 1941. Humphrey Bogart, Lauren Bacall, Veronica Lake, Barbara Stanwyck, and others appeared in film noir—a genre of downbeat, often despairing crime thrillers. Many film noir (literally "dark film") movies were based on the crime novels of Raymond Chandler. John Wayne starred in westerns and war movies. Also in the 1940s, Alfred Hitchcock moved his movie-making talent to Hollywood, where he turned out stylish chillers such as *Spellbound* (1945), *Notorious* (1946), and *Rope* (1948).

In New York, some of the greatest live theater of the century arrived on Broadway in the 1940s. *A Streetcar Named Desire*, written by Tennessee Williams, opened in 1947. The play explores the volatile relationship between Blanche DuBois, a faded southern belle, and her tough, urban brother-in-law Stanley Kowalski. *Streetcar* won the Pulitzer Prize for drama in 1948 and made a star out of Marlon Brando, who played Stanley in the Broadway cast (and later

on film). *Death of a Salesman* came to Broadway in 1949. Written by the gifted playwright Arthur Miller, this play reveals the tragic underbelly of the American dream through the downfall of traveling salesman Willy Loman. It, too, won a Pulitzer Prize for drama. Eugene O'Neill's *Long Day's Journey into Night* (1940) and John Steinbeck's *The Moon Is Down* (1942) were other complex and gripping dramas of the era.

Musicals played on both stage and screen. The brilliant Richard Rodgers and Oscar Hammerstein wrote the music and words (respectively) for *Oklahoma* (1943), *Carousel* (1945), and *South Pacific* (1949). Legendary songwriter Irving Berlin penned the songs for *This Is the Army* (1942), *Annie Get Your Gun* (1946), and other Broadway shows. Cole Porter weighed in with *Kiss Me Kate* (1948), while the songwriter team of Frederick Loewe and Alan Jay Lerner created *Brigadoon* (1947). After delighting live audiences with their rousing song and dance numbers, these shows moved on to Hollywood and came out as movies.

JOHN WAYNE appeared in more than thirty films in the 1940s, including *Sands of Iwo Jima* (1949) *(left)*, for which he was nominated for an Academy Award.

LENA HORNE sings at a nightclub in 1947.

Hollywood, like the rest of the United States in the early twentieth century, treated African Americans as second-class citizens. On the rare occasions when blacks appeared in the movies, they usually played maids, railroad car porters, other servants, or sometimes Africans in the jungle. The roles were generally racist and demeaning. That's the atmosphere that Lena Horne encountered when she moved to Hollywood in the late 1930s.

Horne had begun her show business career in her native New York City. In 1933, at the age of sixteen, she began dancing and singing at the Cotton Club, a famous nightclub in Harlem, an African American neighborhood in New York. Horne then became a solo singer with a mostly white band.

Horne's next stop was Hollywood, where she signed a contract with Metro-Goldwyn-Mayer (MGM). She was the first African American ever signed to a long-term studio contract. At first, MGM gave Horne small, often uncredited roles. Her big break came in *Stormy Weather,* an all-black musical from 1943. After that, she worked steadily. By the mid-1940s, Horne was the highest-paid African American actor in Hollywood.

Horne usually played an entertainer. Sometimes, when her movies screened in the racially segregated South, distributors cut the film and spliced it back together to eliminate her performances. Once, when Horne was scheduled to sing at a military base in Arkansas, she looked out at the audience and saw that the African American GIs were sitting in the back row, behind the German prisoners of war. Outraged, Horne walked off the stage and sang directly for the African American troops.

In the 1950s, Horne's career ran dry. During this era of anti-Communist hysteria, the studios branded her a Communist sympathizer and blacklisted her. No one would hire her to act, so she returned to singing in nightclubs. In the early 1960s, Horne joined the fight for African American civil rights. She continued to sing, act, and make records through the rest of the century. In the twenty-first century, she is still a beloved artist.

JUDY GARLAND appeared in more than twenty films in the 1940s, including classic musicals such as *Easter Parade* and *Meet Me in St. Louis (right)*.

■ OUT WITH THE OLD . . .

Since the 1920s, radio had been a staple in U.S. households. In many homes, families gathered around the living room radio after dinner just as modern families watch television. People listened to news, music, and sports. Serial dramas followed characters from one cliffhanger to the next. Comedy-variety shows featured songs and jokes. Soap operas were over-the-top serial melodramas. During and between shows, listeners heard advertisements from "commercial sponsors"—the companies that paid to put the shows on the air.

Situation comedies were popular radio fare. *Fibber McGee and Molly, Duffy's Tavern, The Great Gildersleeve,* and *Our Miss Brooks* were just a few of many 1940s comedy favorites. *The Lone Ranger* serial followed the travails of a masked western hero and his Indian sidekick. *You Bet Your Life* was a quiz show hosted by Groucho Marx, best known for making movie comedies with his three brothers. Singer Kate Smith had a popular weekly

105

❝ The American Broadcasting Company presents the *Candid Microphone,* the program that brings you the secretly recorded conversations and reactions of all kinds of people in all kinds of situations. No one ever knows when he's talking into the candid microphone. ❞

—Candid Microphone *radio show opener, 1947*

GEORGE BURNS AND GRACIE ALLEN perform their CBS radio show in 1949.

radio show. So did George Burns and his scatterbrained (on radio, anyway) wife, Gracie Allen.

When the United States went to war, radio heroes also joined the fight. *Captain Midnight* was a civilian good guy when his radio show first aired in 1938. When war came, he took charge of the Secret Squadron, a military organization that fought Axis bad guys all over Europe and Asia.

■ . . . IN WITH THE NEW

After the war, radio had to compete with the newest entertainment technology: television. Put on hold during the war years, television arrived boldly after World War II. In 1946 about ten thousand U.S. homes had TV sets. When RCA broadcast the 1947 World Series as an experiment, people without television sets of their own rushed to bars and appliance store windows to watch televisions there. Once people had a taste of television, TV sales jumped. By 1951 twelve million U.S. homes had televisions.

In the late 1940s, television programming was limited to just a handful of evening shows. But when the TV was on, viewers—especially children— were riveted to the set. Popular shows included the *Texaco Star Theater*, a comedy-variety show starring Milton "Mr. Television" Berle; children's favorite *Howdy Doody*, with its human and puppet cast; *The Philco Television*

Playhouse, which broadcast live dramas; and *Toast of the Town*, a variety show with host Ed Sullivan.

Many shows jumped from radio to television between the 1940s and early 1950s. These crossovers included family comedies (*The Goldbergs, Father Knows Best*, and *The Adventures of Ozzie and Harriet*), crime dramas (*Dragnet*), and *Candid Microphone* (which became *Candid Camera*). People kept listening to radio for news and music. But since it projected images as well as sounds, television put on a better overall show. Many serial radio programs didn't make for good television and went off the air.

The Academy of Television Arts and Sciences handed out the first Emmy Awards in 1949. The U.S. public never looked back. From then on, the flickering television screen ruled their living rooms.

Americans of the late 1940s bought **CONSUMER GOODS**, including newly available televisions.

BENNY GOODMAN conducts his orchestra in 1944.

CHAPTER NINE

"MUSIC, MUSIC, MUSIC"
SONG AND DANCE

For a night on the town in the early 1940s, nothing beat live music. At ballrooms and nightclubs across the country, Americans gathered to hear the hottest big bands. The big bands, emerging from the earlier swing bands of the 1930s, featured big brass, woodwind, and percussion sections. The music was jazzy, lush, and danceable. Often a solo singer performed with the band.

Benny Goodman, Jimmy Dorsey, Tommy Dorsey, Glenn Miller, Harry James, and Artie Shaw were among the era's most famous bandleaders. Jo Stafford, Peggy Lee, Doris Day, Helen Forrest, and Dinah Shore were some of the beloved "girl singers" who traveled with the bands. Hits of the era included "Chattanooga Choo Choo" and "In the Mood" from Glenn Miller's orchestra and "Take the A Train" from Duke Ellington.

In the segregated United States, big bands were pioneers because they sometimes featured black and white musicians playing together. Many top bandleaders, most notably Duke Ellington, were African Americans. In addition, many black singers toured with the bands. For example, Sarah Vaughn and Ella Fitzgerald started their careers as band singers and then went on to solo fame.

JITTERBUGGIN'

When the band started playing in the early 1940s, the kids started dancing. They packed into ballrooms and social clubs to "cut a rug." The basic dance was the jitterbug, which had arrived in dance halls in the late 1930s. Partners held hands and then swirled and spun their way through a variety of fancy footwork. When the music got more romantic, dancers

109

snuggled up closer for waltzes and other slow dances.

The USO frequently sponsored canteens, or social gatherings, for stateside troops. There, lonely GIs could dance with local young women—usually under the watchful eyes of older chaperones. If the dancers were lucky, they jitterbugged to a live band. But if need be, a jukebox (record player) was a suitable substitute.

In New York, the hottest big bands played at the Stork Club, 21, the Rainbow Room, and Toots Shor's. Bands also regularly left New York, taking their shows on the road to smaller cities across the nation. People everywhere could hear plenty of big band music on the radio. *Spotlight Band* was a fixture of wartime radio. The show featured the nation's hottest big bands, playing live at military bases, defense plants, and other venues.

■ "PRAISE THE LORD AND PASS THE AMMUNITION"

After the Japanese attack on Pearl Harbor in 1941, songwriters churned out patriotic tunes to inspire Americans during wartime. Some of these songs, such as "Goodbye, Momma, I'm Off to Yokohama" and "Praise the Lord and Pass the Ammunition," were quite popular. Others, including "Let's Knock the Hit out of Hitler," never really caught on.

A U.S. soldier and his partner **DANCE THE JITTERBUG** in 1943.

THE ANDREWS SISTERS—*(from left)* Maxine, Patty, and Laverne—sang in terrific three-part harmony.

Patty, Maxine, and Laverne Andrews were three talented sisters who sang in close harmony. They recorded some of the most beloved wartime hits. Their "Boogie-Woogie Bugle Boy" told about a soldier who spiced up his military bugle calls with boogie-woogie rhythms. "Don't Sit under the Apple Tree" had a soldier imploring his sweetheart to be faithful while he was away at war.

Like other patriotic Americans, bandleader Glenn Miller wanted to fight the Axis. He disbanded his orchestra and joined the U.S. Army during World War II. But he didn't put down his trombone and pick up a gun. Instead, he led the U.S. Army Air Force Band, which played for soldiers at bases around Europe. In 1944 Miller's plane disappeared on a flight from London to Paris, where he was scheduled to play a show. Most likely, the plane crashed into the English Channel. But no wreckage was ever found, and Miller's exact fate remains a mystery.

■ CROON AND SWOON

"He was a skinny kid with big ears," remembered Tommy Dorsey. "And yet what he did to women was something awful. And he did it every night, everywhere he went." He was Frank Sinatra. And what he did was sing. When "the Voice" took the stage, young women in the audience wept, screamed, and swooned. Sinatra was the nation's first teen heartthrob. His teenage fans were called bobby-soxers because of their rolled, ankle-high socks (usually worn with penny loafers). Sinatra was twenty-four when he joined Harry James's band in 1939. From 1940 to 1942, he toured with Tommy Dorsey. He soon became more popular than the bands he sang with. He launched his own solo career in 1943. He also acted in movies.

FRANK SINATRA *(right)* records with Tommy Dorsey *(left)* in 1941.

Sinatra sang in a soft, sexy style called crooning. He was a hot ticket, and soon every band wanted a crooner. Perry Como, Dean Martin, Nat King Cole, Eddie Fisher, Vic Damone, and Mel Tormé were soon also crooning their way to fame. Despite the competition, Frank Sinatra remained the King of Swoon (according to his press agent).

■ VARIETY

Big bands and jitterbug dominated in the early 1940s, but they never drowned out other kinds of music and dance. Bob Wills had a popular western swing band. It mixed swing music with country and featured lots of fiddling. Gene Autry acted and sang in movie westerns, thus earning the title the Singing Cowboy. He also had hits with noncowboy numbers, such as "Rudolph the Red-Nosed Reindeer" in 1949. In the late 1940s, Alabaman Hank Williams introduced a hard-driving country sound that picked up steam in the following decade. Earl Scruggs, Lester Flatt, and Bill Monroe were pioneering bluegrass musicians. They played country tunes on fiddles, banjos, guitars, and mandolins, often at breakneck speed and with vocalists singing close-pitched harmonies.

Chicago had an active blues music scene, spearheaded by guitarist Muddy Waters, harmonica player Sonny Boy Williamson, and others. New York City seemed like an unlikely place for old-fashioned folksinging, but it was there that Woody Guthrie, Pete Seeger, and other folksingers drew large crowds. Meanwhile, an African American singer named Mahalia Jackson combined blues, jazz, and religious music to create a powerful new gospel sound in the 1940s. Her 1947 recording of "Move on up a Little Higher" sold more than one million records and earned her the title the Gospel Queen. Many Americans enjoyed classical music, opera, and ballet in the 1940s. *Appalachian Spring*, a joyful ballet choreographed by Martha Graham with music by Aaron Copland, thrilled audiences when it debuted in Washington, D.C., in 1941.

■ BOP

Toward the end of World War II, big band music began to decline. With many men serving in the military, it was sometimes hard for bandleaders to find enough talented musicians to staff their orchestras. When the soldier/musicians returned

1940s PROFILE: Johnny Mercer

Behind every great singer there's a great songwriter, and in the 1940s, that songwriter was likely to be Johnny Mercer. Mercer was born in Savannah, Georgia, in 1909. As a boy, he sang in his church choir. He wrote his first song at the age of fifteen.

Mercer dreamed of moving to New York, the center of U.S. show business, and he made it there in the late 1920s. He landed a job singing with a big band in 1932. Then his songwriting career also took off. He wrote songs for big bands, movies, and Broadway, often teaming up with Harold Arlen, Hoagy Carmichael, and Jerome Kern.

In the early 1940s, he hosted his own radio show, *Johnny Mercer's Music Shop,* and in 1942, he founded Capital Records. The radio show, record label, and Mercer's own compositions helped propel the careers of Peggy Lee, Frank Sinatra, Nat King Cole, Billie Holiday, Judy Garland, and other U.S. musical legends.

Mercer's hit songs of the 1940s include "Fools Rush In" (1940), "That Old Black Magic" (1942), "Ac-cent-Tchu-Ate the Positive" (1944), and "Come Rain or Come Shine" (1946). He continued to write songs throughout the 1950s and 1960s. By the time he died in 1976, Johnny Mercer had written more than one thousand songs.

from war in the mid and late 1940s, they were often more interested in settling down with their families than in traveling with a band. In addition, Americans turned their attention to new entertainments in the late 1940s, especially television.

"The bebop people have a language of their own. . . . Their expressions of approval include 'cool'!"

—New Yorker *magazine, 1948*

Meanwhile, jazz music itself was changing. In the early 1940s, in the smoky clubs of Harlem, trumpeter Dizzy Gillespie, saxophonist Charlie "Bird" Parker, pianist Thelonious Monk, and others played around with a new, innovative sound. The music, known as bop, or bebop, didn't follow predictable rhythms or patterns. Instead, the players peppered their tunes with unexpected changes in melody, unusual chords and notes, and long improvised solos.

By the late 1940s, bebop had replaced big band as the music of choice for jazz lovers. The African American bebop musicians began to attract a young white audience. A new youth culture started to jell around the bebop sound. Bebop's innovative rhythms soon inspired young writers, such as Jack Kerouac and Allen Ginsberg, to use similar innovations in prose and poetry.

BEBOP MUSICIANS Tommy Potter (bass), Charlie Parker (saxophone), Miles Davis (trumpet), and Duke Jordan (piano) perform at the Three Deuces Club in New York in 1947.

Billie Holiday, born in Baltimore, Maryland, in 1915, was perhaps the greatest jazz singer of the twentieth century. Music historians aren't certain about her early life. Most of what they do know comes from Holiday's autobiography, which is thought to be largely inaccurate. But it is certain that young Holiday was very poor and that she moved from Baltimore to New York City in her teens.

In 1930 Holiday began singing in New York nightclubs. In 1933 record producer John Hammond heard her sing in a Harlem club. Impressed, Hammond arranged for her to record with the famous bandleader Benny Goodman. Under Hammond's guidance, Holiday's career took off. She performed and recorded regularly with some of the greatest jazz musicians of the era, including bandleaders Count Basie and Artie Shaw.

In 1939 Holiday recorded "Strange Fruit," a song written by New York schoolteacher Abel Meeropol. The song denounced the routine lynching of black men by whites in the southern United States. With its serious social message, "Strange Fruit" was unlike anything else in jazz at the time. It won Holiday more acclaim and more listeners.

BILLIE HOLIDAY *(center, at microphone)* sings for a crowd in 1942.

By the mid-1940s, Holiday was a major recording star. Her voice was sharp edged yet sweet. In songs such as "God Bless the Child" and "The Man I Love," she frequently veered away from the rest of the musicians, embellishing a melody line like a jazz instrumentalist playing a solo.

Holiday's life began to crumble in the late 1940s. She became addicted to drugs and drank heavily. Although she continued to perform, her health and her vocal abilities declined. In 1956 she published her autobiography, *Lady Sings the Blues*. In 1959, at the age of forty-four, she died of heart disease and complications of drug use.

115

JOE DIMAGGIO gets a record-breaking hit in 1941. His single broke the record for hitting safely in consecutive games.

CHAPTER TEN
AMERICA'S GAMES:
SPORTS IN THE 1940s

I n the 1940s, the U.S. sports scene was more limited than it is in modern times. Professional baseball had only sixteen teams. Professional basketball was brand new. Professional football had only thirteen teams and a small fan base. But that doesn't mean Americans weren't sports crazy in the 1940s. Baseball—both major and minor league—was part of the nation's lifeblood. The sport was nicknamed America's pastime. Baseball fans packed into hometown stadiums and listened to games on radio. People also followed college football closely. Boxing and horse racing were other popular sports of the decade.

■ FOR THE DURATION

The most exciting baseball event of the early 1940s took place in the summer of 1941, when "Joltin' Joe" DiMaggio of the New York Yankees hit safely in a record-setting fifty-six games. That same year, Ted Williams of the Boston Red Sox reached another milestone by hitting .406 for the season (no big-league player has hit over .400 since).

But with war raging in Europe, DiMaggio, Williams, and other baseball stars wondered what might be in store for professional sports in the coming years. The 1940 Olympic Games had been canceled. The Wimbledon tennis championships, played in Great Britain, had shut down too. What would happen to U.S. sports if the United States entered the war?

When war did come late in 1941, baseball stars quickly joined up. Williams, DiMaggio and his brother Dom, Phil Rizzuto, Hank Greenberg, Pee Wee Reese, Schoolboy Rowe, and other players traded in their team uniforms for military duds. In all, more than four thousand of about fifty-seven hundred professional baseball players joined the armed forces. Most minorleague teams shut down completely.

In 1942 baseball commissioner Judge Kennesaw Landis considered canceling major-league ball for the duration of the war. He asked President Roosevelt's opinion. Roosevelt knew that Americans needed to take their minds off the fears and deprivations of wartime—and that baseball could offer that distraction. He answered Landis: "Baseball provides a recreation which . . . can be got for very little cost. . . . Players are a definite recreational asset to . . . their fellow citizens—and that in my judgment is thoroughly worthwhile." He concluded, "I honestly feel it would be best for the country to keep baseball going."

So baseball did keep going, but it wasn't the same game. The players who hadn't gone to war were old and slow. Fans kept coming, but the action on the field was less than stellar. The same kind of decline occurred in college and pro football. Most of the athletic young men were overseas or training to go there. Only the military academies fielded decent college football teams in the early 1940s.

Joe Louis, the heavyweight boxing champ, joined the army in 1942. He didn't fight the enemy but instead gave exhibition boxing matches for his fellow soldiers. Other top boxers joined the armed forces as well, leaving nothing but no-talent fighters to compete. So boxing officials said forget it. They decided not to hold any title bouts until Louis and the other champions returned from war.

BOXER JOE LOUIS *(second from right)* greets other soldiers at Fort Meade, Maryland, in 1943.

In the early twentieth century, women's sports got little attention and even less funding. There were no professional leagues for women. Neither schools nor society encouraged female athletics. None of that stopped Babe Didrikson. Her real name was Mildred, but when she slugged a baseball like a pro as a little girl, people started calling her Babe, after superslugger Babe Ruth.

Didrikson was born in Port Arthur, Texas, probably in 1911. She played basketball and golf in high school and then played amateur basketball in Dallas, Texas. Next, she took up track and field and quickly dominated Amateur Athletic Union events. That success led her to the 1932 Summer Olympics, where she earned two gold medals (in javelin and hurdles) and a silver (in the high jump). She also set two world records at the 1932 Olympics.

Didrikson returned to golf in 1933. She was an instant star, regularly hitting the ball 250 yards (229 m), equal to the hitting power of male players. When asked how she hit so far, she replied, "You've got to loosen your girdle and let it rip."

Although she also competed in basketball, baseball, swimming, diving, billiards, and tennis, Didrikson focused on golf through the 1930s and 1940s. She racked up a string of amateur tournament wins. In 1945, 1946, and 1947, the Associated Press named her the Female Athlete of the Year. In 1947 she won seventeen of the

BABE DIDRIKSON swings a golf club in 1948.

eighteen tournaments she entered. That year she turned pro. She dominated in professional golf as she had in amateur play. She and fellow golfer Patty Berg founded the Ladies Professional Golf Association in 1949.

Didrikson was diagnosed with cancer in 1953. Despite her illness, she continued to play—and win—professional golf tournaments. Didrikson died in 1956. She is remembered as the greatest female athlete of the first half of the twentieth century.

■ "GIRLS" PLAY BALL

Philip K. Wrigley owned the Chicago Cubs baseball team and ran the Wrigley chewing gum company. He was distressed about baseball's wartime decline. He wanted to keep the crowds coming into his Wrigley Field, where the Cubs played their home games.

So Wrigley and his fellow baseball executives came up with a plan. Why not let professional women's teams play in big-league ballparks on days when regular men's teams were on the road? Women were already building bombers in defense plants. Women's amateur softball leagues flourished across the country. Surely, women could play baseball too, Wrigley reasoned.

Wrigley's plan took shape in the spring of 1943. Organizers recruited the best female ballplayers in the United States and Canada. They modified

Members of the 1945 **ALL-AMERICAN GIRLS PROFESSIONAL BASEBALL LEAGUE** pose in their uniforms.

softball rules to make the game more like baseball. The league's original name was the All-American Girls Softball League. It went through several name changes before finally ending up as the All-American Girls Professional Baseball League (AAGPBL). Instead of playing in big-league parks as Wrigley had planned, the teams played mostly in minor-league parks in small midwestern towns. There, games were well attended. Fans followed their local teams with gusto.

> **"Boyish bobs are not permissible and in general your hair should be well groomed at all times with longer hair preferable to short hair cuts. Lipstick should always be on."**

—All-American Girls Professional Baseball League "Rules of Conduct," rule number 2, 1943

The AAGPBL players were talented athletes. But Wrigley and his fellow organizers wanted to show fans that players were not too brash, tough, or tomboyish. Despite the heroic work of Rosie the Riveter and her colleagues on the assembly line, Americans of the 1940s still had strict ideas about how women should dress, talk, and behave. So Wrigley hired cosmetics manufacturer Helena Rubinstein to run an evening charm school for his athletes. They learned about makeup, manners, and "ladylike" dress and behavior. The league imposed strict rules of conduct, and chaperones supervised players in their free time. Few players complained about the rules and regulations. They were making good money—up to $85 a week for the best performers. Playing baseball professionally was a dream job that many young women were eager to land.

■ BACK IN BUSINESS

When World War II ended in 1945, professional sports returned to prewar standards. In stadiums and athletic fields across the country, fans could once again watch their favorite ballplayers doing what they did best.

JACKIE ROBINSON *(right)* stands in the dugout with fellow 1947 Dodger infielders *(from left)* John Jorgensen, Pee Wee Reese, and Ed Stanky.

Like much of U.S. society, professional baseball was segregated in the first half of the twentieth century. Major-league ball was for white players only. Blacks were restricted to the Negro Leagues, which received little press attention. Because of segregation, the greatest African American baseball players of the century couldn't show their skills on a national stage.

In the 1940s, Branch Rickey, general manager of the Brooklyn Dodgers, wanted to sign an African American player and thereby integrate the major leagues. He knew that the player he chose would endure racial taunts and worse. He wanted a player who could not only stand up to the racist backlash but also perform at the top level of play. Rickey's choice was Jackie Robinson.

Robinson had been a star athlete at the University of California in Los Angeles, both in baseball and football. He had joined the Negro Leagues in 1945. The following year, Robinson made the first step in integrating baseball by signing with the Montreal Royals, a minor-league team. On April 15, 1947, Robinson played his debut game with the Dodgers in Ebbets Field in Brooklyn, New York.

As expected, the reaction was explosive. Some fans jeered, taunted, and threatened Robinson. Some players shunned him or kicked him with spiked shoes as he ran the bases. But *Life* and *Time* magazines put his picture on their covers. Integrating baseball was major news. Just eleven weeks after Robinson's first big-league game, Larry Doby, another African American athlete, debuted with the Cleveland Indians. Other teams quickly integrated their rosters.

Jackie Robinson lived up to Rickey's expectations—and then some. He batted .297 in his rookie year, won National League Rookie of the Year honors, and led his team to the 1947 World Series. He played with the Dodgers for ten years, winning a string of honors, including the National League's Most Valuable Player award in 1949. In 1962 Robinson was the first African American player inducted into the Baseball Hall of Fame.

In 1948 the Olympic Games resumed after a twelve-year suspension. But as punishment for their wartime aggression, Germany and Japan were not allowed to send athletes to the Olympics. At the Summer Games in London, American Bob Mathias won the gold medal in the decathlon—a ten-event track-and-field contest. At the Winter Games in Saint Moritz, Switzerland, Dick Button of the United States took home a gold in figure skating.

Stateside, 6 foot 10 inch (208 cm) George Mikan was burning up the court in college and then professional basketball. Sam Snead dominated in men's professional golf, while Babe Didrikson and Patty Berg led the women's field. A horse named Citation won horse racing's Triple Crown (winning the Kentucky Derby, the Preakness Stakes, and the Belmont Stakes) in 1948.

In baseball, however, business did not proceed exactly as usual. On April 15, 1947, Jackie Robinson became the first African American baseball player signed to a major-league team. Some racist baseball fans were angry. Others hailed the change as a major step for equality for African Americans. Professional basketball and professional football were integrated about the same time. But baseball—the nation's pastime—was much more popular, so Robinson's achievement made headlines around the world.

CITATION *(left)*, ridden by Eddie Arcado, wins the Belmont Stakes and the Triple Crown on June 12, 1948.

Thousands of people in Times Square in New York City CELEBRATE THE SURRENDER OF JAPAN on August 15, 1945.

NEW WORLD ORDER

I
t's impossible to separate the 1940s from World War II. The war colored the entire decade, even the peacetime years of 1946 to 1949. After the war ended, Americans found themselves profoundly changed. Some had lost sons, husbands, and brothers on the battlefields of Europe and Japan. Others had moved clear across the country to take jobs in new wartime industries. Women had discovered skills and strengths they had never before been able to explore. African Americans, having been given a chance to show their abilities in the military, were eager to expand on civil rights gains at war's end. Japanese Americans were bitter about their imprisonment during the war. They too were eager to fight for justice and equality in the late 1940s.

World War II influenced writers, who reflected on their wartime experiences in novels and memoirs. It created a whole new genre of war movies, as well as songs and other forms of expression. On the home front, the war brought Americans together with a unified spirit and sense of purpose rarely seen before or since.

■ SHOCK WAVES

In the postwar 1940s, the United States flexed its muscles mightily on the world stage. On the battlefields of Europe and Asia, U.S. fighters had proved themselves to be strong,

125

brave, and fair—and the nation intended to continue in this role, whether in fighting the Soviet Union, assisting the war-torn nations of Europe, or leading the United Nations.

But there was a darker side to the postwar era. When they were revealed at war's end, the killings of the Holocaust (mass slaughter by the Nazis) shocked the world. People everywhere vowed that such genocide would never happen again. The Holocaust also convinced the world that the Jews—the majority of Hitler's victims—needed a homeland of their own. The State of Israel, created in 1948, was that homeland.

The dropping of atomic bombs on Hiroshima and Nagasaki was equally profound. The utter destruction of the two cities and the horrific deaths of their citizens convinced many people that nuclear weapons should never again be used. A movement to ban nuclear weapons began in the United States in the 1950s.

> **When they were revealed at war's end, the killings of the Holocaust shocked the world. People everywhere vowed that such genocide would never happen again.**

PRISONERS AT THE NAZI CONCENTRATION CAMP IN DACHAU, GERMANY, rejoice as the U.S. Army comes to liberate them in 1945.

ELEANOR ROOSEVELT, wife of President Franklin Roosevelt, was the U.S. representative to the United Nations from 1945 to 1952 and from 1961 to 1962. Here she holds a copy of the Universal Declaration of Human Rights.

Although most people cheered World War II as a "good war"—a fight to save the world from Fascism—others had more complicated reactions. The war led many people to question the human capacity for brutality. Dwight Eisenhower, who saw Holocaust victims firsthand, later wrote to his wife, "I never dreamed that such cruelty, bestiality, and savagery could really exist in this world." In 1945 people around the world were determined to use the new United Nations to prevent further savagery. The preamble to the UN Charter vowed:

> We the peoples of the United Nations determined
> - to save succeeding generations from the scourge of war, which twice in our lifetime has brought untold sorrow to mankind, and
> - to reaffirm faith in fundamental human rights, in the dignity and worth of the human person, in the equal rights of men and women and of nations large and small, and
> - to establish conditions under which justice and respect for the obligations arising from treaties and other sources of international law can be maintained, and
> - to promote social progress and better standards of life in larger freedom,

And for these ends
- to practice tolerance and live together in peace with one another as good neighbors, and
- to unite our strength to maintain international peace and security, and
- to ensure, by the acceptance of principles and the institution of methods, that armed force shall not be used, save in the common interest, and
- to employ international machinery for the promotion of the economic and social advancement of all peoples,

Have resolved to combine our efforts to accomplish these aims.

Accordingly, our respective Governments, through representatives assembled in the city of San Francisco, who have exhibited their full powers found to be in good and due form, have agreed to the present Charter of the United Nations and do hereby establish an international organization to be known as the United Nations.

THE UNITED STATES went through a huge baby boom following World War II. Returning soldiers married, had children, and settled into new suburban homes. The economy flourished.

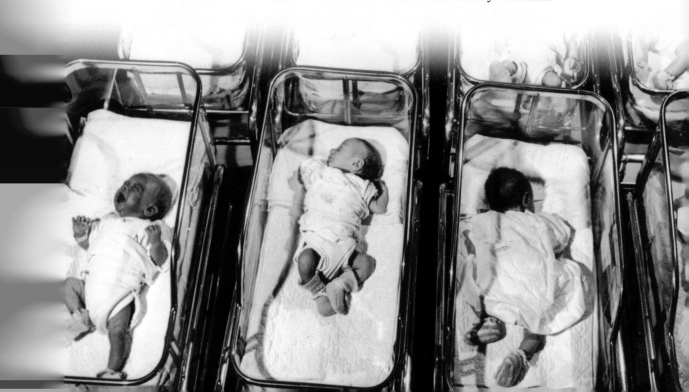

THE AUTO INDUSTRY SURGED as the U.S. economy boomed after World War II.

◼ HAPPY ENDING

In the decades following World War II, many artists and writers examined the war's dark side. In the 1960s, for instance, novelists Joseph Heller and Kurt Vonnegut exposed the absurd aspects of the war in satirical novels. But in the late 1940s, on the streets of the new U.S. suburbs, most people didn't spend much time ruminating about the war and its larger meanings. They were mostly eager to enjoy the peace.

Americans went on something of a spree in the late 1940s. The Depression was over. World War II was over. It was finally a time to celebrate and enjoy the best that life had to offer. And there was so much to enjoy: plentiful jobs, a baby boom, new suburban homes, time-saving appliances, television sets, big new cars, medical advances, and the confidence and pride that came from having defeated Fascism around the world.

One American woman spoke for many when she summed up her feelings from the late 1940s. It felt as if "good times were going to go on and on," she said. "Everything was going to get better. It was just a wonderful happy ending."

1940

- Germany invades Denmark, the Netherlands, and France.
- The United States creates the Selective Service System to draft men into the military.
- Richard Wright's *Native Son* is published.
- Grandma Moses holds a one-woman art show in New York City.
- Warner Brothers introduces Bugs Bunny cartoons.

1941

- The Japanese attack Pearl Harbor, Hawaii, and the United States declares war on Japan.
- President Franklin Roosevelt signs Executive Order 9066, authorizing the relocation of Japanese Americans to prison camps in western states.
- NBC and CBS make the first television broadcasts from New York City.
- Lincoln Borglum completes the carvings on Mount Rushmore in South Dakota.
- *Citizen Kane* plays in movie theaters.
- *Appalachian Spring* debuts in Washington, D.C.

1942

- U.S. and Filipino troops endure the Bataan Death March in the Philippines.
- Allied forces invade North Africa.
- Food and gasoline rationing begins in the United States.
- U.S. automakers stop producing passenger cars
- Kodak introduces color film for personal cameras.
- *Casablanca* plays in movie theaters.
- The Andrews Sisters record "Don't Sit under the Apple Tree."

1943

- Physicists begin building a nuclear bomb in Los Alamos, New Mexico.
- Selman Waksman discovers a cure for tuberculosis.
- *Here Is Your War* by war correspondent Ernie Pyle is published.
- Norman Rockwell's *Rosie the Riveter* appears on the cover of the *Saturday Evening Post*.
- *Oklahoma* debuts on Broadway.
- The All-American Girls Professional Baseball League plays its first season.

1944

- The Allies invade Normandy (France) on D-day.
- Congress passes the GI Bill.
- *Seventeen* magazine debuts.

1944
- *Lifeboat* plays in movie theaters.
- Johnny Mercer writes "Ac-Cent-Tchu-Ate the Positive."

1945
- Germany surrenders to the Allies in May.
- The United States drops atomic bombs on Hiroshima and Nagasaki, and Japan surrenders.
- The United Nations is created.
- The Nuremberg Trials of nazi war criminals begin in Germany.
- Joe Rosenthal photographs the flag raising on Iwo Jima.
- *The Story of G.I. Joe* plays in movie theaters.

1946
- Airlines offer round-trip flights from New York City to Paris.
- The baby boom officially begins on January 1.
- Benjamin Spock's *Common Sense Book of Baby and Child Care* is published.
- *The Best Years of Our Lives* plays in movie theaters.

1947
- President Harry Truman creates the Central Intelligence Agency.
- The House Un-American Activities Committee investigates suspected Communists in Hollywood.
- Test pilot Chuck Yeager flies faster than the speed of sound.
- *Howdy Doody* debuts on television.
- Jackie Robinson integrates professional baseball.

1948
- President Truman desegregates the U.S. military.
- The United States creates the Marshall Plan to help Europe rebuild after World War II.
- Polaroid introduces the Land Camera.
- *Other Voices, Other Rooms* by Truman Capote is published.
- *Texaco Star Theater* and *Toast of the Town* debut on television.
- Citation wins the Triple Crown of Thoroughbred Racing.

1949
- The United States and European nations form the North Atlantic Treaty Organization.
- The Academy of Television Arts and Sciences gives out the first Emmy Awards.
- Philip Johnson builds the Glass House in Connecticut.
- Babe Didrikson and Patty Berg found the Ladies Professional Golf Association.

6 Mark Jonathan Harris, Franklin Mitchell, and Steven Schechter, *The Homefront: America during World War II,* introduction by Studs Terkel (New York: G. P. Putnam's Sons, 1984), 20.

10 Lorraine Glennon, ed., *Our Times: The Illustrated History of the Twentieth Century* (Atlanta: Turner Publishing, 1995), 302.

11 Ibid.

11 PBS, "MacArthur's Speeches: 'I Shall Return'" *American Experience,* 2009, http://www.pbs.org/wgbh/amex/macarthur/filmmore/reference/primary/macspeech02.html (March 30, 2009)

13 Eric Bergerud, *Touched with Fire: The Land War in the South Pacific* (New York: Viking, 1996), 70.

14 Ibid.

16 Dwight D. Eisenhower, *Crusade in Europe* (Garden City, NY: Doubleday and Company, 1948), 225.

16 Ibid.

17 NPR, "Edward R. Murrow: Broadcasting History," *National Public Radio,* May 6, 2004, http://www.npr.org/templates/story/story.php?storyId=1872668 (October 16, 2007).

18 Robert Leckie, *The Wars of America* (New York: Harper and Row, 1987), 794.

18 Ibid., 798.

19 Dan Van der Vat, *D-Day: The Greatest Invasion—A People's History* (Toronto: Madison Press Books, 2003), 83.

20 Richard B. Stolley, *Events That Shaped the Century* (New York: Time-Life Books, 1998), 102.

20 Leckie, *The Wars of America,* 294.

21 Ibid., 107.

25 Rachel Fermi and Esther Samra, *Picturing the Bomb: Photographs from the Secret World of the Manhattan Project* (New York: Harry N. Abrams, 1995), 195.

25 *National Atomic Museum,* "Nagasaki," *National Atomic Museum,* 2003, http://www.atomicmuseum.com/tour/dd5.cfm (October 16, 2007).

27 John Baylis, *Ambiguity and Deterrence: British Nuclear Strategy 1945–1964* (New York: Oxford University Press, USA, 1995), 37.

29 B. D. Zevin, ed., *Nothing to Fear: The Selected Addresses of Franklin Delano Roosevelt, 1932–1945* (New York: Houghton Mifflin, 1946), 454.

29 Ibid.

33 Smithsonian National Museum of American History, "Cold War," *National Museum of American History,* n.d., http://americanhistory.si.edu/militaryhistory/printable/section.asp?id=11 (October 16, 2007).

37 Ibid.

39 Jeff Hughes, *The Manhattan Project: Big Science and the Atom Bomb* (New York: Columbia University Press, 2002), 65.

41 PBS, "J. Robert Oppenheimer (1904–1967)," *American Experience: Race for the Superbomb,* 2007, http://www.pbs.org/wgbh/amex/bomb/peopleevents/pandeAMEX65.html (October 16, 2007).

42 William Manchester, *The Glory and the Dream: A Narrative History of America 1932–1972,* vol. 1 (Boston: Little Brown, 1974), 66.

42 PBS, "J. Robert Oppenheimer."

43 Manchester, *The Glory and the Dream,* 66.

47 Adclassix.com, "1947 United Airlines," *Adclassix.com,* 2008, http://www.adclassix.com/ads/47united.htm (July 15, 2008).

51 Robert S. McElvaine, *The Great Depression: America, 1929–1941* (New York: Times Books, 1993), 186.

54 Roy Hoopes, *Americans Remember the Home Front* (New York: Berkeley Books, 2000), 273.

55 Harris, Mitchell, and Schechter, *Homefront,* 158.

59 Hoopes, *Americans Remember the Home Front*, 241–242.

63 National Park Service, "A Generation of Leadership—Third Term," *Franklin Delano Roosevelt Memorial*, 2004, http://www.nps.gov/fdrm/memorial/room3.htm (November 15, 2007).

64 Hoopes, *Americans Remember*, 36.

66 PBS, "The Good War and Those Who Refused to Fight It," *Public Broadcasting Service*, 2008, http://www.pbs.org/itvs/thegoodwar/ww2pacifists.html (November 5, 2008).

72 Ibid., 273.

72 Harris, Mitchell, and Schechter, *Homefront*, 215.

73 Ibid.

73 Glennon, *Our Times*, 342.

80 United States Holocaust Memorial Museum, "Fighting the Fires of Hate: America and the Nazi Book Burnings," *usmm.org*, n.d., http://www.ushmm.org/museum/exhibit/online/bookburning/war.php (October 17, 2007).

80 James Tobin, *Ernie Pyle's War: America's Eyewitness to World War II* (New York: Free Press, 1997), 184.

84 Raymond Chandler, *The Big Sleep* (1939; repr., New York: Vintage Books, 1988), 42.

84 Raymond Chandler, *Farewell, My Lovely* (1940; repr., New York: Vintage Books, 1992), 93.

84 Ibid., 238.

88 Mitchell Landsberg, "Fifty Years Later, Iwo Jima Photographer Fights His Own Battles, *Associated Press*, 2007, http://www.ap.org/pages/about/pulitzer/rosenthal.html (October 16, 2007).

93 Metropolitan Museum of Art, "Timeline of Art History," *metmuseum.org*, 2008, http://www.metmuseum.org/TOAH/hd/abex/hd_abex.htm (July 15, 2008).

96 John Woolley and Gerhard Peters, ed., "Address at the Dedication of the Thomas Jefferson Memorial, Washington, D.C.," *American Presidency Project*, 2007, http://www.presidency.ucsb.edu/ws/index.php?pid=16383 (October 16, 2007).

102 Steven Mintz, "World War II and Film," *Digital History Resource Center*, 2004, http://www.class.uh.edu/mintz/places/film-9_ww2.html (November 5, 2008).

105 WebRing, "Candid Microphone," *Free Old Time Radio Shows*, n.d., http://www.freeotrshows.com/otr/c/Candid_Microphone.html (October 16, 2007).

111 Glennon, *Our Times*, 324.

114 Steve Lohr, "Ideas and Trends; It's Hot, Has Four Letters and Legs," *New York Times*, July 27, 1995, http://query.nytimes.com/gst/fullpage.html?res=990CE4D61F3FF934A1575BC0A963958260&sec=&spon=&pagewanted=all (July 15, 2008).

118 Richard Lingeman, *Don't You Know There's a War On: The American Home Front, 1941–1945* (New York: G. P. Putnam's Sons, 1970), 326.

118 Glennon, *Our Times*, 312.

119 Larry Schwartz, "Didrikson Was a Woman Ahead of Her Time," *ESPN.com*, n.d., http://espn.go.com/sportscentury/features/00014147.html (October 16, 2007).

121 AAGPBL, "League Rules of Conduct," *All-American Girls Professional Baseball League*, 2005, http://www.aagpbl.org/league/conduct.cfm (October 16, 2007).

127 Eisenhower Memorial Commission, "Ike and the Death Camps," *Dwight D. Eisenhower Memorial Commission*, 2004, http://www.eisenhowermemorial.org/stories/death-camps.htm (November 5, 2008).

127–128 UN, "Charter of the United Nations," *United Nations*, 2008, http://www.un.org/aboutun/charter/ (November 5, 2008).

129 Harris, Mitchell, and Schecter, *Homefront*, 256.

SELECTED BIBLIOGRAPHY

Alperovitz, Gar. *The Decision to Use the Atomic Bomb—and the Architecture of an American Myth.* New York: Alfred A. Knopf, 1995.
Did the United States need to drop atomic bombs to win the war in the Pacific? Many Americans, including President Harry Truman, believed so. Others have argued that the United States dropped the bombs mainly to demonstrate its power to the Soviet Union. Here, Alperovitz offers a detailed exploration of the decision to use the bomb.

Bergerud, Eric. *Touched with Fire: The Land War in the South Pacific.* New York: Viking, 1996.
Bergerud tells the story of the Pacific theater through the eyes of the fighters on the ground. He interviewed dozens of veterans, who relate their stories of fierce jungle warfare.

Eisenhower, Dwight D. *Crusade in Europe.* Garden City, NY: Doubleday and Company, 1948.
General Dwight D. Eisenhower (later president of the United States) commanded the Allied forces in Europe during World War II. In this book, he tells the story of the war as he experienced it—from Pearl Harbor to North Africa, from D-day to the war's end and aftermath.

Fermi, Rachel, and Esther Samra. *Picturing the Bomb: Photographs from the Secret World of the Manhattan Project.* New York: Harry N. Abrams, 1995.
Rachel Fermi is the granddaughter of Enrico Fermi, one of the lead physicists with the Manhattan Project, which developed the first atomic bomb. Fermi and Samra explore the project using words and photographs. Many of the photographs come from scientists' personal collections and show day-to-day life at Los Alamos, New Mexico; Oakridge, Tennessee; and Hanford, Washington.

Glennon, Lorraine, ed. *Our Times: The Illustrated History of the Twentieth Century.* Atlanta: Turner Publishing, 1995.
This terrific book examines the twentieth century year by year, with coverage of art, politics, sports, and entertainment. Colorful photographs and illustrations bring history to life.

Goodwin, Doris Kearns. *No Ordinary Time: Franklin and Eleanor Roosevelt: The Home Front in World War II.* New York: Simon and Schuster, 1994.
Award-winning historian Doris Kearns Goodwin examines the World War II years through the eyes and experiences of the most famous Americans of the era—President Franklin D. Roosevelt and his wife, Eleanor.

Harris, Mark Jonathan, Franklin Mitchell, and Steven Schechter. *The Homefront: America during World War II.* Introduction by Studs Terkel. New York: G. P. Putnam's Sons, 1984.
The authors interviewed dozens of Americans about their World War II home front experiences. In their own words, the interviewees explain life in wartime. They discuss defense work, Japanese relocation, blackouts, and more.

Hartmann, Susan M. *American Women in the 1940s: The Home Front and Beyond.* Boston: Twayne Publishers, 1982.
The 1940s was a dramatic decade for American women. While caring for their homes and families, they also stepped in to work when men went off to war. Women's wartime experiences gave them a new sense of their own economic and political power. This book examines this pivotal period in U.S. women's history.

Hughes, Jeff. *The Manhattan Project: Big Science and the Atom Bomb.* New York: Columbia University Press, 2002.
Hughes traces the twentieth-century quest to build an atomic bomb. He examines the Manhattan Project, the destruction of Hiroshima and Nagasaki at the end of World War II, and the postwar explosion of science in the United States.

Jenkins, Alan. *The Forties.* New York: Universe Books, 1977.
Jenkins explores 1940s culture: art, fashion, sports, music, and more. Although he focuses on Great Britain, he also looks at trends in the United States.

Leonard, Thomas M. *Day by Day: The Forties.* New York: Facts on File, 1977.
This massive book examines the 1940s on a day-by-day basis. Using a tabular format, the author looks at every day of the decade and lists the major events in world affairs, World War II, and U.S. culture, policy, politics, and leisure.

Lingerman, Richard R. *Don't You Know There's a War On? The American Home Front, 1941–1945.* New York: G. P. Putnam's Sons, 1970.
This fascinating title reveals the war behind the war—life on the U.S. home front. Lingerman explores how various groups—children, women, blacks, and whites—contributed to defeating the Axis. He examines rationing, war bonds, defense jobs, civil defense, wartime entertainment and propaganda, and other home front efforts.

Tobin, James. *Ernie Pyle's War: America's Eyewitness to World War II.* New York: Free Press, 1997.
Tobin chronicles the life of the man who chronicled World War II. That man was Ernie Pyle, who lived, worked, and died alongside the ordinary GIs who fought the war.

Van der Vat, Dan. *D-Day: The Greatest Invasion—A People's History.* Toronto: Madison Press Books, 2003.
The author chronicles the D-day invasion in meticulous detail. Photographs, maps, and eyewitness quotes combine to convey the urgency, terror, and exhilaration of June 6, 1944.

Books

Allman, Toney. *J. Robert Oppenheimer.* Farmington Hills, MI: Blackbirch Press, 2005.
Physicist Robert Oppenheimer was the reluctant father of atomic warfare. He led the project to build the first atomic bomb but later spoke out about the dangers of atomic warfare. Readers will learn about his scientific work as well as his political views.

Bradley, James. *Flags of Our Fathers: Heroes of Iwo Jima.* New York: Delacorte Books for Young Readers, 2001.
John Bradley was one of six men who raised the U.S. flag on Mount Suribachi during the battle for Iwo Jima in 1945. James Bradley, his son, tells about his father and the other five flag raisers, Joe Rosenthal's famous photograph of the event, and how U.S. leaders used Rosenthal's image as propaganda. This book is the young people's edition of Bradley's longer work for adults.

California Historical Society. *Only What We Could Carry: The Japanese American Internment Experience.* Berkeley, CA: Heyday Books, 2000.
One of many tragedies of World War II was the unjust treatment of Japanese Americans by the U.S. government. Using poetry, fiction, news stories, government documents, photographs, and illustrations, this book presents a thorough picture of Japanese American evacuation and relocation during the war.

Gourley, Catherine. *Rosie and Mrs. America: Perceptions of Women in the 1930s and 1940s.* Minneapolis: Twenty-First Century Books, 2008.
This book looks at U.S. women through the lenses of advertising, magazines, movies, radio, and other popular media. In the 1940s, the "Rosie the Riveter" stereotype took hold. Yet women were still expected to be demure and traditionally feminine. Gourley's insightful book explores both the stereotypes and the reality of women's lives in the Depression and World War II eras.

Josephson, Judith Pinkerton. *Growing Up in World War II, 1941 to 1945.* Minneapolis: Lerner Publications Company, 2003.
You didn't have to be a soldier to fight during World War II. Even children helped win the war by collecting scrap rubber and metal, buying war bonds, and planting victory gardens. This book tells the stories of U.S. children during wartime.

Lawton, Clive A. *Hiroshima: The Story of the First Atomic Bomb.* Cambridge, MA: Candlewick Press, 2004.
The bombing of Hiroshima was a horrific event that changed the course of history. Here, the author examines the event in great detail—from the race to build the first bomb to the destruction it wrought to the arms race that followed. Black-and-white and full-color photos illuminate the text.

Lazo, Caroline Evensen. *Harry S. Truman.* Minneapolis: Twenty-First Century Books, 2003.
Harry Truman took over the U.S. presidency when Franklin Roosevelt died in 1945—just as World War II was ending. Under Truman's leadership, the United States dropped atomic bombs on Japan

and confronted Communism at home and abroad. This book explores Truman's life, work, and legacy.

Oliver, Clare. *Jackson Pollock.* New York: Franklin Watts, 2003.
In the 1940s, a new artistic movement emerged in the United States. That movement was abstract expressionism, and its leader was Jackson Pollock. Here, readers will learn how the painter dripped and splattered his way into the art history books.

Roberts, Jeremy. *Franklin D. Roosevelt.* Minneapolis: Twenty-First Century Books, 2003.
Franklin Roosevelt steered the nation through the Great Depression and World War II. The only president to serve more than two terms, he was greatly beloved. But his presidency was not without controversy. This book explores his personal and political journey.

Robinson, Sharon. *Promises to Keep: How Jackie Robinson Changed America.* New York: Scholastic, 2004.
Jackie Robinson was the first African American man to play baseball in the major leagues, and Sharon Robinson is his daughter. She tells her father's story using news and family photos, quotes from newspapers and magazines, and other primary sources. Readers will learn about segregated baseball and how Robinson helped usher in a new era in race relations.

Sherman, Josepha. *The Cold War.* Minneapolis: Twenty-First Century Books, 2004.
The Cold War emerged at the end of World War II, when the United States broke with its former ally the Soviet Union. In the United States, Communism became the new enemy—and even innocent Americans were suspect. This book looks at the Cold War from its early roots to its late twentieth-century demise.

Viola, Kevin. *Joe DiMaggio.* Minneapolis: Twenty-First Century Books, 2006.
Baseball was "America's game" in the 1940s—and the king of the diamond was Joe DiMaggio of the New York Yankees. He accomplished his famous fifty-six-game hitting streak in 1941, left baseball to join the army, and returned to his winning ways after the war ended. In this Sports Heroes and Legends biography, readers will learn about this baseball great and why Americans loved him.

Whitman, Sylvia. *Uncle Sam Wants You! Military Men and Women of World War II.* Minneapolis: Lerner Publications Company, 1993.
Nearly 16 million Americans served in the military during World War II. This book examines the day-to-day life for those on the front lines and those behind the scenes. Using interviews with veterans, songs, slogans, and historic photographs, Sylvia Whitman tells the soldiers' stories.

———. *V Is for Victory: The American Home Front during World War II.* Minneapolis: Lerner Publications Company, 1993.
World War II involved more than just soldiers on the battlefield. Ordinary Americans took part by working in defense plants, buying war bonds, and saving scrap metal and rubber. With photographs and firsthand accounts, this book examines the struggles and victories on the home front.

Williams, Barbara. *World War II—Pacific.* Minneapolis: Twenty-First Century Books, 2005.
This comprehensive title explores World War II in the Pacific theater—from Pearl Harbor to the
Battle of Midway to the bombing of Hiroshima and Nagasaki. Williams details the battles, the
fighting forces, the weapons, and the home front in wartime.

Films

Fly Girls. DVD. Boston: WGBH Boston, 2006.
Part of the PBS *American Experience* series, this film sheds light on a little-known group from
World War II: the Women's Airforce Service Pilots. These women tested military airplanes, trained
male pilots, and ferried aircraft and cargo. Using interviews and archival footage, the film tells
their stories.

Television: Window to the World. DVD. New York: A&E Television Networks, 2005.
After decades of trial and error, television finally made it into U.S. homes after World War II.
It immediately transformed U.S. culture and family life. This interesting documentary traces
the early history of television—with a special emphasis on the inventors and broadcasters who
struggled to make it a reality.

The War. DVD. Arlington, VA: Public Broadcasting Service, 2007.
Director Ken Burns is the master of documentary history, and here Burns outdoes himself. This
six-disc, fifteen-hour documentary shows World War II through the eyes of those who experienced
it. Burns examines families on the home front as well as soldiers in the field. He uses letters,
interviews, and archival and family films to reveal the brutal realities of war.

Websites

The Good War and Those Who Refused to Fight It
http://www.pbs.org/itvs/thegoodwar/story.html
Using pictures and interviews, this site chronicles the experiences of conscientious objectors
during World War II. The site is a companion to a PBS film of the same name.

Sinatra
http://www.sinatra.com
The first teen heartthrob, Frank Sinatra sent young women screaming when he sang with Tommy
Dorsey's band in the early 1940s. Sinatra reflected the decade's style in his songs, movies, and
clothing. This website celebrates his life and work.

SELECTED 1940s CLASSICS

Books

Mailer, Norman. *The Naked and the Dead.* 1948. Reprint, New York: Henry Holt, 1998.
Critics have called Mailer's book the greatest novel about World War II. The story follows the struggles of a fourteen-man infantry platoon as they try to survive on a Japanese-held South Pacific island.

McCullers, Carson. *The Heart Is a Lonely Hunter.* 1940. Reprint, Santa Barbara, CA: Landmark Books, 1988.
This moving tale, set in a small Georgia town in the 1930s, centers on the friendships and struggles of a deaf man named John Singer. The book has been hailed as a literary masterpiece and earned great acclaim for McCullers, who was just twenty-three when it was published.

Wright, Richard. *Native Son.* 1940. Reprint, New York: Harper Perennial Modern Classics, 2005.
Wright's protagonist is Bigger Thomas, a young African American man living in the slums of Chicago. Driven by poverty and despair, Thomas commits murder and receives a death sentence. A best seller, the book helped shed light on racism and injustice in U.S. society.

Films

Casablanca. DVD. Burbank, CA: Warner Home Video, 2000.
Humphrey Bogart and Ingrid Bergman star in this drama, set in Casablanca, Morocco, during World War II. With the Nazis on their trail, Ilsa Lund (Bergman) and her husband Victor Lazlo (Paul Henreid) need to escape Casablanca. But Isla's love for her old flame Rick Blaine (Bogart) holds her back.

Citizen Kane. DVD. Atlanta: Turner Home Entertainment, 2001.
Orson Welles directed and starred in this classic U.S. film. It tells the story of Charles Foster Kane, a newspaper tycoon based on real-life publisher William Randolph Hearst. Acclaimed for its sound track, lighting, camera angles, editing, and storytelling, the film broke old rules and set new standards for filmmaking.

Double Indemnity. DVD. Universal City, CA: Universal Studios, 2006.
Raymond Chandler wrote the script for this film noir classic, directed by Billy Wilder. Barbara Stanwyck and Fred McMurray star as a pair of scheming lovers out for a fat insurance payoff. First, they commit murder—then they turn on each other.

Identify six to ten things in your own life, neighborhood, or family history that relate to the 1940s. (For ideas, consider your town, grandparents' or neighbors' lives, family antiques or collections, your house or buildings in your hometown, movies, books, songs, TV shows, or places you've visited that connect to the 1940s.) Use photographs, mementos, and words to create a print or computer scrapbook of your 1940s connections.

INDEX

143

ABOUT THE AUTHOR

Edmund Lindop has written many books for young adults, including several books in the Decades of Twentieth-Century America series.

Margaret J. Goldstein was born in Detroit and graduated from the University of Michigan. She is an editor and author for young readers. She lives in Santa Fe, New Mexico.

PHOTO ACKNOWLEDGMENTS

The images in this book are used with the permission of: © Express/Hulton Archive/Getty Images, pp. 3, 72–73; Franklin D. Roosevelt Presidential Library, pp. 4–5, 30, 81; © Hulton Archive/Getty Images, pp. 6, 92, 102; AP Photo, pp. 7, 17, 22, 26–27, 38–39, 48, 66, 78, 96, 106, 111, 112, 116–117, 122, 123; National Archives, pp. 8–9 (W&C 1134), 10 (W&C 0743), 12–13 (W&C 1145), 19 (W&C 1040), 20–21 (W&C 1041), 25 (W&C 1358), 28 (W&C 1296), 54 (W&C 0800), 56 (W&C 0792), 69 (210-62-C153), 70 (W&C 0921), 86–87 (W&C 1221), 89 (W&C 0798), 90 (W&C 0827), 124 (W&C 1359), 140 (top right) (W&C 1358); AP Photo/USMC via National Archives, p. 15; Library of Congress, pp. 23 (LC-DIG-ppmsca-13260), 44 (LC-USW33-042469), 50–51 (LC-USW33-028624-C), 58 (LC-USZC2-1142), 65 (LC-DIG-fsac-1a34555), 82 (LC-USZ62-42506); © SuperStock, Inc./SuperStock, p. 24; AP Photo/stf, pp. 31, 41, 94; AP Photo/apn, p. 33; © Keystone/Hulton Archive/Getty Images, p. 34; © Al Fenn/Time & Life Pictures/Getty Images, p. 35; © New York Times Co./Hulton Archive/Getty Images, p. 36; © Ed Clark/Life Magazine/Time & Life Pictures/Getty Images, p. 40; © Los Alamos National Laboratory/Time & Life Pictures/Getty Images, p. 42; © Bettmann/CORBIS, p. 46; © Topical Press Agency/Hulton Archive/Getty Images, pp. 47, 140 (bottom); U.S. Air Force photo, p. 49; © William Vandivert/Life Magazine/Time & Life Pictures/Getty Images, p. 52; © Hansel Mieth/Time & Life Pictures/Getty Images, p. 53 (both); © Howard Hollem/Anthony Potter Collection/Hulton Archive/Getty Images, p. 57; © Myron Davis/Time & Life Pictures/Getty Images, p. 59; © Brown Brothers, p. 61; © Anthony Potter Collection/Hulton Archive/Getty Images, pp. 62–63; © Alfred Eisenstaedt/Time & Life Pictures/Getty Images, p. 64; © Alfred Eisenstaedt/Pix Inc./Time & Life Pictures/Getty Images, p. 67; © Mark Kauffman/Time & Life Pictures/Getty Images, p. 71; © Shelly Grossman/FPG/Hulton Archive/Getty Images, pp. 74–75; © US Army/Time & Life Pictures/Getty Images, pp. 76–77; © Carl Mydans/Time & Life Pictures/Getty Images, p. 79 (left); © J. R. Eyerman/Time & Life Pictures/Getty Images, p. 79 (right); © DC Comics, Inc., p. 80; © Lisa Larsen/Time & Life Pictures/Getty Images, p. 83; © Ralph Crane/Time & Life Pictures/Getty Images, p. 84; © Morgan Collection/Hulton Archive/Getty Images, p. 85; Printed by permission of the Norman Rockwell Family Agency Copyright © 1943 Norman Rockwell Family Entities. Image provided by Library of Congress (LC-USW33-023859-C), p. 91; © Martha Holmes/Time & Life Pictures/Getty Images, p. 93; © Nina Leen/Time & Life Pictures/Getty Images, p. 97; MGM/The Kobal Collection, pp. 98–99; Warner Bros/The Kobal Collection/Woods, Jack, p. 100; Republic/The Kobal Collection, p. 103; © Yale Joel/Time & Life Pictures/Getty Images, p. 104; © MGM Studios/Hulton Archive/Courtesy of Getty Images, p. 105; © George Karger/Time & Life Pictures/Getty Images, p. 107; © Wallace Kirkland/Time & Life Pictures/Getty Images, pp. 108–109, 120; © Keystone Features/Hulton Archive/Getty Images, pp. 110, 140 (top left); © Frank Driggs Collection/Hulton Archive/Getty Images, p. 114; © Gjon Mili/Time & Life Pictures/Getty Images, p. 115; AP Photo/Henry Griffin, p. 118; © Diamond Images/Getty Images, p. 119; © Horace Abrahams/Hulton Archive/Getty Images, p. 126; UN Photo, p. 127; © Three Lions/Hulton Archive/Getty Images, p. 128; © Frank Scherschel/Time & Life Pictures/Getty Images, p. 129.

Front Cover: U.S. Air Force photo (top left); Library of Congress (LC-DIG-fsac-1a35312) (top right); © Mark Rucker/Transcendental Graphics/Getty Images (bottom left); Library of Congress (LC-USZ62-25600) (bottom right).